Mothering
Through
Bipolar

Rebecca Moore

Booktrope Editions
Seattle, WA 2015

Cover Design by Gwen Gades
Edited by Elaine Papciak

Previously published 2014 Createspace

PRINT ISBN 978-1-62015-873-9
EPUB ISBN 978-1-62015-904-0
Library of Congress Control Number: 2015905405

*If you or someone you know is in crisis, stop reading this right now
and call 911 or your local, crisis hotline. Remember suicide is a
permanent solution to a temporary problem*

*Disclaimer: Any information provided in this book is based on my own personal experiences and opinions.
No information provided in this book should ever replace the opinions and advice of a professional. I am not
a doctor, psychiatrist or affiliated with any mental health organization. I ask you to please consult with
your own physician before you decide to use my opinions or information for your own personal use.*

Acknowledgments

I'd like to thank the team at Booktrope, Katherine Fye Sears, Jesse James and Jennifer Paul Gilbert for believing in *Mothering Through Bipolar* and giving me a chance. A special thank you to *Team Mothering Through Bipolar*, Elaine Papciak, my wonderful dear friend and editor for helping me to put my heart and soul into *Mothering Through Bipolar*. To Gwen Gades for the beautiful cover design that makes *Mothering Through Bipolar* stand out. To Melissa Flickinger for jumping in with both feet and taking on the task of proof reader and to my awesome book manager Jamie Greene! Thank you all so much for your hard work and dedication! I couldn't have done it without you!

Dedicated to my children:
Danny, Andrew, Lizzie,
Joshua, Gracie, Emma,
And
Mollie

I am a bipolar mom to seven wonderful children. Dan and I have been together since high school. He has seen my ups and my downs; my good times and my bad times, and he has always loved me through it. Most of the years we've been together I have gone undiagnosed and wrongly medicated. Without the support from Dan and our children I would not have come as far as I have.

I was properly diagnosed when I was 33-years-old, but I know I have always been bipolar. I just didn't recognize the signs. There was no label slapped on me to define or name the issues I had been experiencing. Everyone else around me knew, they just didn't know how to approach the situation. I have come to realize that I was a bipolar mom before I ever was diagnosed as having bipolar disorder. Having that knowledge has allowed me to step outside of my diagnosis and realize that nothing has changed. I now have a label that describes a certain set of symptoms I experience, but I do have choices. I can either let my diagnosis consume me and control every aspect of mine and my family's lives, or I can choose to learn how to manage my mental illness and remain well for myself and my family. I have decided to choose the latter of those two. There is always a reason to keep fighting, no matter how small that reason seems to be.

My hope through writing this book is to help others out there, like myself, who struggle daily with parenting while having bipolar disorder. I know how difficult it is to be a parent with a severe mental disorder. Trying to keep up, care for your kids and care for yourself can sometimes feel insurmountable. I can only hope that my book will be of some support and encouragement for you.

I am also a mother to a child who suffers with a mental disorder herself. She has not been officially diagnosed as of yet, but I am sure that will change once her psychiatrist and therapist have more information. I understand the challenges of raising a child with a mental illness. I hope I can offer some encouragement to you there as well.

My very best wishes,
Becca

embracingmadness.com
facebook.com/rebeccamooreauthor

Chapter One

IT WAS JANUARY 2011 and I was just coming out of one of the worst postpartum depressions I had ever experienced with any of my children. I had experienced postpartum depression with almost every baby I gave birth to, but this time it was different. There was this crushing darkness, the kind that envelopes you and pulls you under. It's like you can see everyone else breathing around you, except you are drowning. I loved my new baby, but I didn't want to care for her. I was tired and worn out and it was crushing me inside to not be able to be the mother I wanted to be. Baby Emmie was an excellent baby, not that there is such a thing as a bad baby. But, she was content and extremely happy, that is once we got past the nursing stage. She was a great nurser, but one who wanted to nurse ALL the time. Taking care of her five older siblings, trying to keep the house clean and organized, doing laundry and homeschooling two of her siblings was taking its toll on me. I just didn't have the energy left in me anymore to continue nursing her. I was only sleeping at best two hours a night and those two hours were spent in a rocking chair. That just wasn't cutting it for anyone in our home and my mood was suffering horribly. Three weeks in and the decision was made, we were switching Emmie over to formula. I had nursed all my babies, even through the postpartum depression, but this time I just couldn't do it anymore. I felt completely inadequate as a mother. I didn't want to care for her and now I didn't want to feed her. I was losing my grip on what it was like to be the mother I once was.

There was an immediate difference in Emmie. She was sleeping through the night. She took a long nap in the afternoon and she was only eating every three to four hours. Emmie was every mother's dream. She was and still is the perfect baby. There was one problem though. I still wasn't feeling perfect. I had bouts of anger coming from nowhere. Things, little things, like shoes being left in the middle of the floor or toys being played with after I cleaned up, all started to get on my nerves. I found myself snapping at those around me. Their behavior, their voices were annoying me. I began fights with Dan over everything and anything. Soon followed the blame game. This is where I began blaming everyone around me for conspiring against me or doing things to purposely hurt me. It's not fun for anyone around me and when I come out of this, I'm embarrassed and filled with humiliation.

I still felt tired and worn down and was having a terrible time keeping up. It shouldn't have been this way. Emmie was eating and sleeping wonderfully and so was I. Everyone in the house was getting the proper amount of sleep. I should have felt refreshed after a good night of sleep. Instead, I felt like I hadn't slept in a month. I was groggy and needed naps during the day to keep going. It was then that Dan suggested something that sounded so awful, I wanted to cry. "What if you are pregnant again?" he said to me. I just stared through him. There was no possibility he was right! Emmie was only a few months old, I had been nursing, there was no way I could be pregnant again. I wasn't emotionally ready, let alone physically ready to have another child. I didn't even know if I wanted to have another child. I was horrified.

That night Dan bought me a pregnancy test and sure enough, I was absolutely pregnant again! After the initial shock wore off, we were both euphoric with excitement! I wasn't so horrified any longer. I was filled with excitement and it felt as though the darkness that had been surrounding me for the last two months was already lifting. There was nothing more exciting than the thought of having another child. Even if that meant another long, terrible postpartum depression. Both of us found it hard to not want to share the news with everyone, but we knew we couldn't, not yet. We already had two pregnancies that had ended before I was even eight weeks along, we needed to keep this to ourselves for a while, just in case. As the weeks ticked by and it became clear that we were definitely having another baby, my excitement grew and so did my stomach. By the time I was three months along, there was no hiding it anymore. Lizzie began asking questions and I couldn't lie to her. Lying to my children was just never an option for me. If they are old enough and mature enough to ask then they are old enough and mature enough to know the answers to the questions they were asking. Lizzie was as ecstatic as we were and she paraded herself around the house singing about being a big sister again. I beamed inside knowing she was a happy girl. It always warmed my heart to see her happy.

The next week we had Children and Youth Services knocking on our door. There were allegations against us that we allowed our oldest son to do things he should not have been doing. I sort of laughed about the situation because anyone who really knows me would know they would not get away with doing something like that to our family. They would have known I wasn't like that, they would have known what could be found in my home and what couldn't be found. They also would have known that Children and Youth always talks to the children and well, children when asked questions unexpectedly, they typically don't lie. Thankfully, a case was never even opened on us. The case worker was very nice, apologized for the inconvenience, recognized the situation as a vindictive call and wrote up her report and handed it in. There was something about that day that changed everything for me. Soon, I was second guessing everything I was doing and had been doing as a mother. Was I staying on top of things like I should be? Was there enough laundry done that it didn't look like a never-ending pile? Was the kitchen clean enough? Were the kids clean enough? If someone close to me would do such a thing as to lie to Children and Youth Services, what else were they capable of doing?

The paranoia began to run rampant through my veins... I jumped every time someone would knock on my door. I found myself peeking through the curtains, always drawn, to see who was outside, who was knocking. If I didn't know them I would take my children into the living room and we would all sit quietly until the intruder went away. I was petrified for my children's safety, sure someone was going to take them away from me or hurt them. Soon the paranoia turned into delusional thinking, except I didn't see it that way. My thoughts were real, my thinking was real and all those people out there in the world, trying to hurt me and my family, were real. One evening, I walked through the house, checked every window and every door. Next, I began grabbing the baseball bats that my children once used to play with outside and put them in each corner of the house. Each corner where I was most likely to be at any given moment. Just in arms reach, so that on a second's notice I could protect myself and my family.

I was certain these people wanted to destroy my life. The best way to do that was through my children and they knew this. I needed to do everything I could to protect them. No longer were they allowed to play outside during the warm, sunny days of summer. They were only allowed to play inside. This confused them and was met with much resistance, but it was the only way I knew how to keep my children close to me and safe. And that's all I cared about, their safety, even if that meant ruining their summer. I just couldn't see the irrational way of my thinking at the time. Everything I was feeling and believing was real in my eyes. I believed with my entire being someone would hurt my children. I truly feared for my children's lives. I began warning my children about constantly keeping the doors locked, they were not to answer the door for anyone. Whenever Dan would leave for work, I would go check and make sure he had locked the door behind him. When Danny would go to his friend's houses, I would yell, "Make sure you lock the door!" and then go check to be sure he listened. Everyone knew not to answer the phone. If it was someone we trusted they would leave a message and we would call them back. Having a relationship with anyone outside of our own four walls was off limits for me. I didn't even like Dan going to work or Danny going down the road to his friend's house. I wanted everyone to stay home with me; I needed to keep everyone safe. When Dan was on-call and would have to leave in the middle of the night, I sat awake, waiting for him, baseball bat by my side. If I heard a noise, I would jump. Sometimes, I would wake Danny in the middle of the night and we'd sit together on the couch and wait for his dad to come home. He would just sit with me, telling me we would be okay; there was nothing to worry about. I was instilling fear into my children's lives without even realizing it. Thank God Dan picked up on a lot of these things. He suggested therapy for me and I took him up on his offer. I needed help; I had enough insight to see that. I knew I needed better coping skills and I needed to stop ruining my children's lives. What I didn't know was that it was going to get worse before it got better.

Talk therapy was not what I needed. I didn't need someone to tell me to forget about all that was happening to me and go on about my life. I knew those things. The problem was, I didn't know how to do those things anymore. Whatever was happening to me sucked whatever rational knowledge I had out of my brain and replaced it with something evil. I needed help with that and my therapist just didn't understand. Her suggestion, medication. She urged me to speak with my OB/GYN about putting me on an antidepressant called Zoloft and I did. Eight weeks into the medication, I was worse off than when I began it. Now, I couldn't even stand to be around anyone. I didn't want Dan home and when he was, I started every fight I could with him.

One night, he and I had a huge fight about his job. It was stupid and ridiculous thinking back over it, but at the time, all I wanted was for him to stay home. I was still overly paranoid and I needed help, I just didn't know how to get it. I also didn't understand that the medication had sent me into a dysphoric mania and I was literally going out of my mind. I took the keys to our van and told Dan I was leaving him. I drove around the neighborhood for about an hour before I the realization set in that I had no place to go. When I came back home, I sat in our driveway until after 2am, the entire time feeling embarrassed and humiliated by my actions. I had said some terrible things to Dan that night, accused him of cheating on me and not really going to work. I was a horrible, wicked person that night. I also wanted to be away from my children, far away. I didn't want to take care of anyone or anything. All I wanted to do was peel my own skin off of my body and if I could have figured out a way to do it, I would have. I wanted to run, faster than I ever had before. Running away seemed like a good option, but where would a pregnant mom of six go? And what would everyone think once she did leave? That's when things really went downhill for me. I started hearing voices, voices telling me how much of a horrible mom I was, how my children deserved better than me. How Dan didn't really love me, he kept me out of obligation. How much of a horrible person I was for all the things that I had done. The voices just wouldn't shut up. I wanted nothing more than to cover my ears and start screaming so I could try and drown them out. But what would my children think? I was teetering between rational and irrational thinking. I needed to get a grip, but the ledge was too far out of my reach.

My thoughts began to drift back to a time that I would love to erase from my mind forever. A friend of the family's had committed suicide. She had two small children at the time and we all wondered how she could do that to them. How could she leave her two children behind without a mother to care for them? We all condemned her without understanding her personal situation. Everyone around her ignored her pleas for help, her struggles were left unnoticed. Eventually, after many medication trials, she decided to put an end to all the suffering. It was in that one moment that I finally understood why she did what she did. It was not done to hurt her children. She loved her children to the moon and back! She did it for the children. She didn't want her children to grow up with a mother who was sick all the time. She wanted better for her children and this was her way of giving it to them. She viewed her death as a gift to them and I was beginning to understand this. I understood it so much that I wanted to give this gift to my own children. I was tired of them seeing me in the state of mind I was in. I was tired of them having to live in fear because their paranoid mother couldn't get it and keep it together. And so, the planning began. Before I acted on the plan, I needed to tell someone about the plan. I don't know why I chose to do this. Part of it may have been because I really didn't want to die. Part of it was because I wanted to live. I wanted to get better, I wanted to stop feeling the way I had been feeling. Next therapy session I let it all out. I cried about the friend I had lost and told my therapist that I wanted better for my children, too. That I understood that this friend was not to be condemned for her actions, but rewarded. That what she had done was an awesome thing for her kids. She did what she knew was best for them.

My therapist sat and listened and then immediately went into action. She explained in detail what my suicide would ultimately do to my children. Where they would end up and what it would do to my husband. She told me that I needed to go inpatient and then she wrote down the number to a Crisis Bed Center. She believed keeping me out of the hospital would be best. I was pregnant and did not need the added stress of being in a locked ward. She felt the Crisis Bed Center would be a better option. She sent me home with instructions to call them immediately and get in as soon as possible.

Chapter Two

I DIDN'T CALL right away. I waited the night out, hoping the feelings would just go away. But every time I closed my eyes, the plan I had just played over and over in my head. The images were not just scary, but there was something eerily calming about them. It was almost like my brain was showing me how it would play out and then the voices started again. Telling me how much I deserved to die. That I deserved this to happen to me. I covered my ears and brought my knees up in bed, laying in a fetal position next to my husband, praying he wouldn't wake up. I needed just a few more hours to pass and then it would be morning. Then I would call. I wouldn't wait, I'd call first thing in the morning. And I did. I spent the entire morning being bounced between agencies. No one knew who I was supposed to call or how to get a referral to the Crisis Bed Center. The number the therapist gave me only directed me to someone else. On my last attempt, I finally got through to someone. This kind lady took all my information: name, address, phone number, date of birth, insurance information. I was psyched because I was finally going to get some help. Then she asked, "Do you have a plan to commit suicide?" I told her yes and then she had me explain what that plan was. Once she heard my plan her voice changed. She wasn't the kind person I was talking to anymore. She wanted to call an ambulance for me, but I begged that she not do that. She instructed me that I had 15 minutes to have my husband home from work or she was calling the ambulance.

There was no way I could allow her to call an ambulance for me. I was alone with my children, I was safe. I wouldn't hurt myself while the kids were around. I did not want my kids to see their mom being taken in an ambulance. I knew what that ride meant, I knew it meant hospitalization and I wanted to avoid a locked ward. I wanted to be treated, to be cared for, not locked in some room and forgotten about. I immediately called Dan and he came home just as the lady from the Crisis Line was calling me back. She instructed me to go straight to the ER, that they were expecting me and that if I didn't go she'd send the police. I did not want to go by force, so I complied with her request.

Dan was absolutely baffled by what was going on. He just didn't understand the extent of what I was going through. I had never told him my feelings or the thoughts I had been having. The only communication we had was through arguments and fighting. He didn't know how horrible it felt to be me. I will never forget the look on my children's faces as they watched me walk out that door. My oldest kept hugging me, telling me I'd be okay. I think he understood even though not a single person had breathed a word to him about what was going on. The others hugged me as well. I could see in their eyes they were afraid for themselves and for their mommy. They were confused. Why was Mommy going to the hospital if she was not sick? All six sets of sad, little eyes followed me as I walked out that door. I had no clue what was about to happen or how long I would be gone. The one thing I did know, I was going to the hospital so I could help myself. I needed to get better; I needed to be the best mom possible. I needed to get the Momma Bear in me back. I needed to protect my children, not from the outside world, but from myself. From their own mommy.

I barely remember the car ride there. I remember getting in the car, but after that is a complete blur. I have no idea as to why this was, but somehow I managed to block the entire car ride out. Maybe it was the finality of actually going. Maybe it was knowing that there was no turning back. Or maybe it was because this would actually make it official. I was crazy and the entire world was going to find out. I was petrified. I had no clue what to expect, what would happen to me. Would they lock me away forever? Were the voices right? Did Dan really want me gone? Was that why he agreed to take me in the first place? Whatever it was, I just don't remember.

Upon arriving at the ER, I think Dan half carried me in there. I couldn't get my feet to move and even if I could, my legs wouldn't cooperate. They were shaking just as badly as my hands were. Once we got inside, I stood partially behind him, my body shaking, my hands trembling, my mind racing. I was doing everything I could to stop myself from hyperventilating. I could hear the small, quiet moans coming from myself and I began to rock on my feet. When we got up to the receptionist area, tears were flowing down my face. I could only whisper three small words, "Crisis Worker, please." I was thankful that I didn't have to go sit in the ER waiting room. I really don't think I could have handled sitting there, a ball of nerves, breaking down in a way that I had never done before. They ushered me right to the back and when the triage nurse took my blood pressure, it was even more of a shock to me. It was extremely high due to the panic attack I was having. I was positive that I was going to have a heart attack and die right before they could do anything to help me. My goal would be accomplished without me even having to do anything.

Next I was taken to a small wing off the side of the ER. Here was a wing, I soon realized, that was reserved for "special" people just like me. A nurse had me quickly go into the bathroom and change out of all my clothes. I was then put in some ridiculous, blue paper suit. Once she was sure I had no weapons on me, she took me to a stretcher that sat in the hallway and I was put on watch. I was stuck between the nurse's station and a small room where the doctors met together. Next I was assigned my own nurse, one who would sit with me through the entire process and watch me like a hawk. There is nothing more humiliating than knowing you are being analyzed, unless, of course, the person analyzing you is someone you went to school with. Just my luck! And of course the first words out of her mouth were, "So, how have things been?" In true bipolar rage fashion I wanted to smack that girl in the mouth, but I was too depressed to do it. Instead I said, "Well, I'm here, aren't I?" After that, she didn't say another word to me. Finally, after two hours a Crisis Worker came to talk to me. They moved me into an empty room and we talked about why I was there. She was very nice, kind and extremely compassionate. Her only downside, she really wanted me admitted and her urgency for this grew once she heard what my plan was. This is when the begging began. I did not want to be hospitalized, I did not want to die, and I just wanted to feel better. I begged for her to let me go home. I repeated over and over, "I just want to go home!' I must have said it at least 25 times throughout our conversation. She continued to insist and I told her the only way I would stay is if I was able to go to the Crisis Bed Center. She insisted there were no beds available for me and that I would have to be hospitalized. This ensued more begging on my part. She eventually asked Dan what he thought. He still wasn't aware of what I had been going through and he was just about to hear what my plan was. When he heard, his eyes got big, but he told the Crisis Worker that he wanted whatever I wanted, and if I wanted to go home he'd take care of me! Dan saying these words showed me that the voices I had been hearing were wrong!

Dan really did love me, he loved me like he had always loved me, if not more. It was the only moment through the entire day that I actually felt some comfort. But there were conditions, there are always conditions.

Dan had to be with me 24-hours-a-day. He was not to allow me to be out of his sight. If I went to the bathroom, the door remained open or he went with me. Dan was unable to return to work until I was in the care of a skilled psychiatrist. Dan was more than willing to follow those rules. I still don't think he understood the extent of what my brain was putting me through. Hell! I didn't even understand. But I knew enough to keep quiet about the voices. If they knew about those, then no matter what I or Dan said, I would not have been going home.

After that, I was basically free. I went into the bathroom, changed out of my paper suit and into my human clothing, happy to be rid of that humiliating outfit. It felt like they were singling me out because I had a mental issue. What I don't think any of them understand is how dehumanizing the entire process is. Although I know it's for safety purposes, I think there are other ways that someone who is in crisis can be treated. The suits are humiliating and having someone go to the bathroom with you is dehumanizing. Adding as little stress to the person who is already having a difficult time is imperative. People who have a bad attitude, who are not compassionate and caring, people who have little to no mental health training should not be caring for those of us who do have a mental health issue. It's this kind of situation that promotes fear in those of us that are seeking help from others. By the time we got home all the younger children were already in bed. I was grateful to my oldest for his help during this time. He stepped up his game and did for us what no one else would do; he cared for his brothers and sisters. My oldest hugged me tightly for a long time, and then he whispered in my ear, "I love you! I would have missed you, Mommy!" He hadn't called me Mommy in years and it was like music to my ears.

That night Dan and I sat up almost all night long. We had a long talk about everything that had been going on. I still don't think he had absorbed the things I was trying to tell him. I don't think he was able to understand how horrible I felt inside. Even I did not understand the storm that had been brewing in my brain. I was baffled by how depressed I was and how everyone and everything around me just made me feel worse. I didn't understand, how could I expect anyone else to? I tried to explain to him how monumental everything was for me. From brushing my teeth to doing the dishes and laundry, it was all just too overwhelming. I just couldn't do it anymore. There was nothing left in me to give. I was nothing.... This information was incomprehensible for Dan. He had always seen me as the high-functioning, get-everything-done-and-keep-everything-in-order kind of gal. I wasn't that person anymore, and I was falling apart in front of him. Like a piece of cracked glass, just one wrong push and I was going to break into a million different, little pieces that no one would be able to glue back together.

The next morning we started making phone calls to every psychiatrist from the ER's list. I was greatly discouraged as I faced this task. We were either expected to wait three months for an appointment, or the doctor was no longer accepting new patients. I finally made an appointment with one of the first doctors I called and decided I had waited this long, what was another three months. There was one number that had a busy signal each time I tried to call it. Something in me told me to try the number again and it rang through this time. The receptionist was kind, compassionate and understanding. She listened to me blubber on about my experience and then told me she had an appointment for that Saturday, just two days after being discharged from the ER. I was ecstatic knowing I didn't have to wait three months. Unfortunately it was just an intake and it would be another three weeks before I could actually see the psychiatrist, but I was okay with that. Three weeks was so much better than waiting three months. Those three weeks flew by because I had Dan home with me. He did so much to help me during that time. I put the kid's homeschooling on hold and lounged around the house. I rid myself of any unnecessary stress.

Chapter Three

THE PSYCHIATRIST I was paired up with after the ER visit turned out to be not so scary. I don't know what I was expecting, but whatever it was, it was not this psychiatrist. Maybe I was thinking certified pill-pusher or someone who needed more help mentally than me, but my psychiatrist was none of those things. He was very thorough when it came to gathering my mental history. Before he even spoke with me, he knew every medication I had already been on and what reactions my body had to those particular medications. He spent about 45 minutes talking with Dan. They covered what life had been like with me through the past 18 years. By the time he was done talking with Dan, I don't think there was much left to ask of me. We went over previous diagnoses and previous failed treatments. He agreed that I absolutely had an anxiety disorder, and that anxiety disorders typically go hand in hand with depression. Then we started talking about mood and if I had ever experienced psychosis. Answering the mood part was easy, psychosis however, well what does that mean? I kind of stared at him blankly. He then started in with some leading questions.

Doc Y: *"Why don't you drive?"*

Me: *"Because I'm scared someone will hit me, I'll hit someone else or someone is following me."*

Doc Y: *"Is there any reason to believe someone is following you?"*

Me: *"No."* There was a long pause before I answered him. I wasn't sure what the correct answer to this question was.

Doc Y: *"Do you think someone wants to hurt you?"*

Me: *"Yes!"* Insert lots of conversation about baseball bats, kids not playing outside, checking doors, keeping drapes closed, and etcetera.

Doc Y: *"Do you think something will happen to your children if you let them outside?"*

Me: *"Yes, someone may kidnap them, hurt them, and yell at them (this one really happened, though), try to use them to hurt me."*

I guess he heard enough at this point, as he spread his hands across his desk and said, "Miss Becca, you can forget about the depression. You have what's called bipolar. Now, here is what we are going to do." I think at that point he realized I was looking at him like he was a ten-headed monster. He told me to go home, educate myself, look it up, read about it, learn about it and come back in a week and tell him what I thought about his diagnosis. So, I did and when I returned a week later, I walked into his office with a completely different attitude. No matter how hard I tried to prove this doctor wrong, I just couldn't! Reading all the symptoms of bipolar disorder described me so well, especially the mixed episodes or what is also known as dysphoric mania. I had been experiencing them for years without even realizing it. Somewhere in there I found a bit of relief. To finally know why I acted the way I did and to know there was actually something that could be done about it. My only regret was not seeking treatment from a psychiatrist earlier. I had instantly wished I had gone back in time and reset the clock. Knowing what I knew then could have stopped a lot of pain for not only me, but the entire family. Once Doc Y knew I wasn't going to argue his stance any longer, he immediately sprang into action. We knew the typical mood stabilizers used for bipolar disorder were not an option. I was almost six months pregnant and most mood stabilizers are not healthy for the baby. He wanted permission to speak with my OB/GYN to discuss treatment options with him. He did not want to prescribe any medications without their prior approval. I gave him my OB's name and telephone number and we began the telephone tag game. Finally after two weeks, we were able to speak with my specialist, a perinatologist whom I had been seeing due to the pregnancy complications I was experiencing, and we received his approval for treatment. He felt that treating me outweighed any risk to the baby and he was absolutely on board with the medication Doc Y had suggested for me.

In an attempt to pare down how much medication I was taking, Doc prescribed me a very low dose of Seroquel. He wanted to try and combat the psychosis, the mood issues, the anxiety, and sleep issues all at the same time. Unfortunately, at 25mg, all I was receiving were the sleep and anxiety benefits. It was not until I hit the 300mg mark when everything else seemed to come together. I was my old self again, for a little while. My brain was finally quiet, I was getting restful sleep and the paranoia and voices were completely gone.

Unfortunately, about a week after hitting 300mg, everything hit me like a ton of bricks. The psychosis returned, the voices were back with a vengeance and I was full of rage. I was not doing well. One day it was so bad I cried to Dan during one of his lunch breaks at home. He offered to take the rest of the day off, but I didn't want him to. I wanted to just run away. I didn't want another person home, in my face, complicating things more than they were. I just wanted to feel normal again. I was so full of the crazies at that point that when I snapped at Joshua, (he was four-years-old at the time), that I realized I wasn't just snapping. Instead, I was screaming at him, full-blown screaming and it was for nothing besides him being your typical four-year-old. Immediately I phoned my psychiatrist's office and got in to see him right away. I told him about what was happening and everything my head was telling me, and he upped my dose to 400mg. That dose saved my life. Within three days I felt a thousand times better. I started to actually care about my life again. More importantly, I started caring about my kids' lives.

The night I started to feel better, Dan was rocking our 10 month old Emmie to sleep. The other children were already in bed and my oldest was spending the night at a friend's house. I had just got done journaling as I do every night before bed. Then I made my way first into our girls' bedroom. I sat on the edge of Gracie Macie's bed and stroked her hair as she slept. Silent tears were streaming down my face. I thought back over the last five years of our lives and all the mistakes and mess ups I had made along the way. How horrible of a parent I had become in such a short amount of time. I realized that my downhill spiral did not just happen that year, but had begun years before - most likely in my teens, but had progressively gotten worse as I got older. All the stress, triggers, the changes and responsibilities added throughout the years only made my bipolar worse and it was only a matter of time before I exploded.

I then thought about how much I loved, adored and cared for my children. How I would do everything in my power to protect them. Protect them from the horrifying side of my illness. My thoughts drifted to how they were the reason that I needed to fight through this and do whatever it took to be as stable as possible. It was for them, not for me, but for my children. That my children were the most important reason for me to do whatever I could to hold it together. That the depression, no matter how debilitating it was, was not going to lie to me any longer. That the depression was not going to make me believe that my children were better off without me. I kissed Macie gently on the forehead, climbed the ladder to kiss Lizzie Girl and walked out of their bedroom.

Next I went into the boys' bedroom. I sat next to Josh for a long time. My illness had probably affected him the most. I had not bonded with him the way I had my other children. His life had been filled with chaos and a very distant mother who took most of her verbal aggression out on him. My tears weren't as silent this time. I tried hard to keep the tone down. I didn't want him to wake up, scared because Mommy was sitting on his bed crying. I ran my fingers through his hair, ran a finger down his cheek and just watched him sleep for a long time. I knew I messed up with him. Now I needed to figure out how to fix it. I kissed him on his forehead and then kissed Andrew. I took one last look back at Joshua, promising myself I would make him feel loved no matter what it took.

I wish I could say everything fell into place. But the truth is, I still wasn't happy with myself or with my life. If I could there would be no reason to continue writing this book. What I can say though is this was a turning point for me. It was what started me to fight and to fight hard. I want other parents to realize there is more to our lives than this diagnosis. Once the medications started to work, so did my brain and I was able to have a completely new perspective into my own life. I could see how my thoughts and actions affected my family. Being in the right mind-set is what enabled me to take action. I was able to view the world and my own life through a clearer set of eyes. I was able to see just how much of my lack of insight had damaged so much of my own life and how the paranoia was generating fear throughout my home. How horribly it affected my children. I just didn't know how to fix the damage that had already begun. How to pick up those tiny puzzle pieces and fit them all together, perfectly, the way they once were. I had to figure out for myself that it wasn't just about making everything perfect, it was about trying my very best to be the mom I once was. That needed to be my primary goal and I needed to work towards that goal. I had to take baby steps and not expect results to happen quickly. I began to make a list of what would help me to remain stable. Some of those things included enrolling Andrew and Lizzie back into public school. Not having to worry about if they were learning enough and not having to deal with the stress that comes with homeschooling, eased a lot off of my mind. I still had fears about sending them back into the public school setting, but most of those fears were residual delusions, part of the psychosis that I needed to learn how to cope with. Once I started poking holes in the delusions I was having, testing them against reality, it was easier for me to see how irrational my thought process was. I spoke with friends and family whom I trusted about this and they all agreed, the children being in school would not only help me, but the kids as well. How were they ever to experience anything if I continued to allow my paranoia to prevent them from living a life?

The next thing on my list was to create a Psychiatric Advanced Directive. Knowing I had my desires for treatment set in place helped me to relax a little. I worried that if I ever found myself incapable of making good decisions, that no one would know exactly how I wanted and needed to be treated. It also helped Dan to know exactly what was acceptable to me and what wasn't. It helped him to understand my needs and wants during a crisis. After that was to stop letting my deluded thinking control my life. This was the hardest part for me, because it seemed so real to me at the time. I had to force myself to open my drapes, and it was a wonderful thing to feel the sunshine warming up a room that I was sitting in. Feeling the sunshine on my face while I journaled or cross stitched, cleaned, or played with the kids was an awesome feeling. It's one that even to this day, I cherish.

A few days later we were handed our eviction notice. I was floored that soon myself and my family were going to be homeless. We had 30 days to find a place to live and I was just two months away from delivering Mollie. This was all due to our inability to pay rent for a few months because Dan needed to be there for me. Most likely, had we explained the situation it may not have gone as far as it had, but I feared that if anyone knew I was diagnosed with bipolar disorder that I would surely lose my children. Had it not been for the Seroquel, I would have had another breakdown. Instead, I looked at the change as a positive step in our lives. One that would allow us much more freedom and independence. I had hopes that I would be able to actually live my life, not just survive. This was a chance for me to rid myself of the extra stress that had been added to my life. It was my first lesson in learning how to keep toxic people away from me, how toxic people can pull us down even when we believe we can't get any deeper in the muddy waters then we already are. It taught me who I could trust and who I couldn't. Yes, this was positive.

It was change I accepted graciously and I went into a full frenzy, getting stuff packed up and sorted. The over-productivity, the amount of packing being done in one day, the rest of the time painting the walls and cleaning the house. Deciding what could go to garbage and what we needed to keep was a daunting, but a necessary one. I'm happy to say, all the packing and moving went smoothly, well as smooth as can be expected from a family of eight, almost nine. I wasn't in the best shape to help all that much, but I tried. After all, I was eight months pregnant and I had another six children to move in the process. But in the end, it all got done and it was probably the best thing we had done in years. Independence is a sweet thing, no matter what price you have to pay to get it.

The move could not have come at a better time.....

Chapter Four

ONCE WE WERE in the new house, I already felt like the weight of the world was lifted off of my shoulders. The unpacking and organizing was done in less than two weeks. The only thing I had left to do was to wash up Baby Mollie's clothes and get her bag packed. I had put this off as the last thing on my list. I wanted to make sure everything else in our home was taken care of first. I found myself working frantically, practically around the clock to get everyone and everything settled.

Everything was set and ready to go. I was looking forward to relaxing for a few weeks before Baby Mollie made her grand appearance into our lives. The only thing left on my to-do list was an OB appointment to set up the scheduled C-section. I had never had one before, but both my psychiatrist and OB agreed it was best. We needed time to set up arrangements for how long Dan could be out of work; time to gather friends who could be a safety net if Dan was unable to remain home for long. It also gave us a chance to prepare for a crisis in the event that things began going downhill after Baby Mollie was born. There was a higher power involved here. Just when I thought I could relax, knowing everything was in place, this higher power proved to me that I had no control over anything in my life or any situation at all. The next day at my appointment, no C-section was set up because I was already in labor, five centimeters dilated and I had absolutely no idea.

My doctor instructed me to go home, pack up the rest of my bags and head straight to the hospital if my contractions got worse or came closer together. He was worried that I would end up delivering at home, and that would cause more stress than delivering in the hospital. I took his advice and did just that. By 7pm I was on my way to the hospital, checked in, still only five centimeters, but the contractions were strong and coming quickly! Thank God for epidurals! There was one problem, though. I had stopped taking my meds about two weeks before Mollie's birth. Partly because I had forgotten about them during the move and partly because I felt so much better, I didn't think I needed them any longer. Even though I had been warned endlessly about NOT doing this, I did it anyway and in the long run, I paid for it. I now know that it was because my mind-set was not where I thought it had been all along. I was not stable and I had no insight into what I was doing. Dan really had no clue until about a week before Mollie made her arrival. He encouraged me daily to take my meds, but I insisted on not taking them. I felt so much better without them. I felt like the old me for a little while and when the paranoia began to creep back in, I kept it to myself because I didn't want to prove anyone right. I didn't want to be on medication. I didn't want my children to grow up with a crazy mother. I had so much internal stigmatization going on. I hated myself for an illness I couldn't control and didn't understand.

Baby Mollie was born quickly and she was healthy as every one of my babies had been. We were worried because of the medications I had taken throughout my pregnancy with her. Other than some jaundice that caused her to spend an extra day in the hospital, she was a perfectly healthy baby. Once she came home, I still didn't start back on the

Seroquel. I thought for sure I was still okay and I could handle it. That doc was wrong and I was fine. Mollie was bottle fed, so that gave me a break when I needed it. Dan was getting up with her a few times at night so I could *try* to get some much needed sleep. But any Mommy knows this is virtually impossible. You hear your baby crying and you are automatically awake. Three weeks after her birth, things fell apart in typical postpartum depression fashion. My mind-set and mood took a significant change for the worse. I found myself in one of the worst mixed episodes I had ever felt. It was very close to the one I had experienced before I was on the Seroquel. Running away seemed like a good option once again. I began fighting with Dan, screaming at the kids, trying to care for a fussy baby, trying to keep the house clean, neat and orderly because everyone knows that a *"good"* mom can do all those things.

But.....I couldn't and soon I was crying about everything and wanted nothing to do with Mollie. I found myself calling Dan, begging him to come home, begging him not to go to work. Begging him to help me because I didn't know how to help myself. Eventually he got the message and came home. He took a leave of absence from work and that's when the real work began. I was back into full-blown psychosis, the voices were louder, I thought about self-harm for the first time, trying to find ways to release all this aggression without putting it on my family again. Remember, it was just a month or so back, I promised myself I'd fight and I had to keep doing that.

I found that I was blaming myself for everything that was going wrong. Dan eventually ended up losing his job and we found ourselves living on half of his regular income, which is not easy when you have seven little people waiting for their meals each night. I had so much self-loathing, I couldn't even stand to look at myself in the mirror. It was my fault that we were in this situation. I was incapable of showering, brushing my teeth, getting dressed, caring for the kids. I was sleeping 14-plus hours a day and still being tired with no motivation, no energy and just wanting to die. Dying wasn't an option, though. I had to keep fighting for the kids. It seemed like an appropriate option under the circumstances. I told Dan, and he and my psychiatrist went into action. Lithium was added to the Seroquel, and daily phone calls from my psychiatrist got me back on track, or so I thought. Unfortunately, not much had changed and I experienced some pretty wacky side-effects with this new combination. Eventually, the Lithium was replaced with Lamitcal. I thought once again that the depression had lifted. I thought I had my mixed episodes under control, I thought the rapid cycling was coming to an end.

I was wrong.

January 2011 rolled around and I felt like I had been holding on by the skin of my teeth. Although the Lamictal had been keeping me out of deep depression, it did not hold me up enough the way the Seroquel had. We tried adding Lithium in with the Lamictal, but I ended up with my gums swelling which caused me to have some major dental issues. As much as I wanted the Lithium to work, it just wasn't meant to be. Unfortunately, this pushed doc and I back to the drawing board. I really needed the depression to be lifted. I was headed to a bad place, one I didn't want to revisit. In an attempt to clear the board, we tried just Lamictal and Klonopin for a little while, but that had less than desirable results.

February I found myself in what I call Hypoland, except I did not recognize it. I thought I was just feeling better. The depression had finally lifted and I thought what I was feeling was normal. My energy increased, I was being more productive, house cleaning and laundry was caught up on. I had motivation again and was ready to get out there and get something done! I even drove the new car, something I hadn't done in over a year. It felt awesome! That right there should have been my first sign that I was headed into dangerous territory. I was going on five hours of sleep, at the most. I'm typically an eight or nine hour person. I was bouncy, giggly and happy. I skipped through parking lots after spending a huge amount of money that we didn't have, humming and singing to myself. I acted like I was five-years-old and my family was taking me to Disney World. The only distinction between the giggly little girl inside of me and the 34-year-old Hypo-maniac was the fact that I craved sex a lot more than I usually had. With all of this combined, and the fact that I actually dyed my hair purple, I'm surprised I didn't see it. But it had been my first mania in a long time and I was loving it!

The purple hair by itself was no big deal, but it definitely tipped my psychiatrist off. I bounced into his office like I was the sexiest person in the place. I sat, practically hopping out of my seat. I was nervous because I was afraid he'd view my happiness as mania and I was in absolute denial that mania was what I was actually experiencing. I just felt like I was living again. I had been so tired of teetering between depression and mixed mania that feeling as good as I felt was amazing. I tried with everything I had to compose myself, I wanted to keep it together long enough to get through our 15 minutes with my psychiatrist. It's sad that the hypo got the best of me, though.

The minute Doc Y opened his mouth; I knew I was in trouble.

Doc Y: *"Ahhh! Miss Becca! The hair!"*

I'm sure had I not been blubbering at the mouth a million miles a minute and giggling like a school girl over a boy she liked he wouldn't have given a hoot about the hair. But I was way too hyper to contain myself and it flowed out of me naturally.

Doc Y: *"So....you seem a little hyper to me?"*

He presented this more like a question then a statement. I think he wanted me to recognize and admit it for myself. Insight was the last thing that I had at that point and all I could do was giggle. Then Doc turned to Dan and I knew I was in big trouble! Dan had been witnessing my behavior for a few weeks and when questioned, Dan would not lie.

Doc Y: *"Has she been hyper, Mr. Dan?"*

Dan: *"Yeah, a little bit!"* Damn! I was caught; there was no turning back now.

Doc Y: *"How's her sleep been?"* Another question that was going to get me into trouble.

Dan: *"Oh! That could definitely be better. She's hardly sleeping at all!"* If I could have duct taped Dan's mouth shut I would have, but I was giggling and smiling so much I doubt I would have been able to unroll the tape.

Doc turned his eyes on me again and proceeded to ask if I thought I was acting a little too hyper. When all I did was giggle he said to me, *"Be honest Miss Becca, are you feeling like you are more hyper than usual?"* Insert lots more giggling from the oblivious hypo-maniac sitting on the couch in her psychiatrist's office. I had no choice but to look away from him. I knew my giggles would turn into laughter. This became increasingly hard, especially when I started to crack some jokes and I looked over at Doc long enough to see that he, too, was giggling to himself. His face turned even a little red! It was then decided that we would give Lithium another try. Fortunately, the Hypoland was demolished before it turned into full mania or I crashed into depression. Unfortunately, I did have the same reaction, lots of gum swelling and dental issues so we had to stop the Lithium once again. Back on the medication merry-go-round we went and this time we landed on Invega, which I thought was the medication from hell. One, my insurance refused to pay for it, so I had been living off of samples. You can only do this for so long when other people need those samples, too. Invega only vaguely diminished the psychosis that typically follows a manic time for me and I was still seeing shadows and hearing voices. We tried upping my dose but I got so restless on it, I couldn't tell if it was even helping with the psychosis. Being on the med merry-go-round is never fun and most of the time you feel like a guinea pig. It is a necessary step towards stability, though. There is no one person that reacts the same to any medication available. Just as some antibiotics work for one person, that same antibiotic may not work for a different person. We are all different and not all meds work the same for each person. Riding the merry-go-round is absolutely beneficial, though. Once you and your doctor find the right mix of meds that work for you, you will be glad you took a few more trips around than you wanted to.

One evening in late April of 2011, I hit one of my lowest points ever. I had been struggling for an entire week about whether I should go inpatient or not. It was a difficult decision as I knew I was not a danger to myself or anyone else, at least not yet. The problem was, I spent that week teetering between mixed mania and depression. I knew if I did not get help soon, I would be in deep depression and it would take someone else intervening for me to get the help I needed. Finally, I made the decision on my own and I'm happy I did.

Chapter Five

WHEN I FIRST WENT inpatient, I was scared to death. I didn't know what to expect. The unknown is always scary, and when putting yourself in a mental health facility, it's no different. The place I went to was amazing. From the staff, to the other residents, to the groups, right down to the structure of this place, I was completely astonished. They were all so caring and supportive. It all left me wondering why every place is not like this one.

The Crisis Team came out to my home to assess me. They spoke with me in length about what I could expect upon arriving at their facility. They also spoke with my husband about my treatment and care and allowed me to have some private time with my children. This gave me the time I needed to explain to my younger children that I was going on a trip and they could even come visit me. Leaving my children was the most difficult part of the entire process. Everything else paled in comparison to leaving my children. I held each of my children and told them not to worry that they could come visit me and I wouldn't be gone long. I promised to call as much as I could. There was something different this time in their eyes. They didn't seem as scared or as confused as they had the first time I had gone to the Emergency Room. This time it was almost like a calm had come over them and they understood that I was doing what was best for everyone.

Upon arrival to the Crisis Bed Center, I was taken immediately into the office and was given an intake. Here I was asked a variety of questions.

Why I was there?

What I expected to get out of the program?

Was I suicidal or homicidal?

Could I contract for safety - meaning would I tell them if I had urges to hurt myself or others?

What were my goals?

How would I rate my depression, anxiety, self-esteem and psychosis? This was done on a rating scale of 1-10....1 being the absolute worse you have ever felt and 10 being the best you have felt. We also went over contact information, insurance information and discussed the services they would provide for me.

After my initial intake was over, it was shift change. They didn't want to have to start me in on a crisis plan only to stop me halfway through, so I was taken to the outside porch where I could smoke and relax. It was here that I met the residents that were currently staying there. They were all so encouraging and promised that this mental health facility would be able to help me. It was almost dinner time, so I jumped in with both feet and helped everyone prepare for dinner. I figured I might as well get used to it as I knew I would be there for a minimum of three days. This was huge for me as I hadn't even cooked a meal for my own family in months, not to mention that somehow the social anxiety I typically would feel around new people seemed to dissipate. I have no doubt that had I been in a locked ward, things would not have been this way. After dinner there was a small break, so that's when I finally got checked into my room. I was fortunate enough to have a private room. This was especially nice as I am a natural introvert and I loved knowing that I had a private place to go recharge when I needed it. My first full day, the nurse woke me early. She gathered all my mental health information and already had all my information from my own psychiatrist. She explained that the psychiatrist I would be talking to that day would also have all this information before he saw me and that his recommendations would be in place before we even met. For some this approach may not be comfortable for them. Some people like to have a lengthy conversation with the doctor that is treating them. This approach doesn't always work well for others, and some residents felt his bedside manner was less than desirable. For me, it was fine. I knew enough about certain medications that if I thought his recommendations were off the wall, I would have said so. I trusted that he would be able to care for me in the appropriate manner for a crisis patient. And he didn't disappointment me. He pushed my Lamictal to 200mg and recommended that my current psychiatrist continue pushing the dose up until we hit 300mg. He felt that Lamictal was the best antidepressant to battle the depression part of my bipolar disorder. He also switched me off of Invega and onto Geodon, 40mg, two times a day, put me on Doxepin for sleep and recommended that I speak with my own psychiatrist about pushing my Klonopin dose to 2mg daily. He was awesome and within 24 hours I was already feeling much better.

There were also three groups held during the day and I think I benefited the most from these groups. Just being surrounded by others who were going through the same things as myself helped in so many different ways. I was able to learn from other people's hindsight. I was able to see past my own depression and feel empathy for others. Being part of these groups helped me to unload a lot that was on my mind and I was able to get different perspectives from all the people surrounding me. These groups offered encouragement, support, guidance and direction. I believe it was during group times that we all bonded collectively.

There was help available to me 24-hours-a-day. At any moment when I needed someone to talk to, there was someone there. Whether that person was a resident or a therapist, there was always an ear to listen to me. When it came time for Dan and the kids to leave, there was always someone there to hug me as I cried and remind me why I was staying. They always kept me in check. During my stay, I worked through many self-help worksheets. There were videos I could watch as well, but I don't learn that way. I need to read, take notes, write and re-read in order to gather the information I need to help myself. I can't watch a video about it because I start to lose concentration. It was through these worksheets that I learned the most about relaxation techniques and how they can help me during times of stress or when I'm in a mixed episode. They taught me what was me, and what was my illness - a distinction I was unable to make prior to working it out on paper. I still use these CBT worksheets now that I am home and well. I also completed my Wellness Recovery Action Plan, while I was inpatient and walked out of there with a list of goals of how I would get through each day.

The most valuable service to me was the aftercare. My family and I were facing eviction at the time of my discharge. The Case Manager made sure that I had telephone numbers for every agency that could potentially help me. He also worked on an insurance issue I was having and set me up for case management services for after discharge. I received a telephone call from the crisis line each night until I knew I was stable enough to trudge along by myself. I cannot thank them enough for not throwing me to the wolves and leaving me to fend for myself.

If you are already considering going inpatient then it's a good chance you probably should go. It took a full week of me teetering between mixed mania and depression before the flip finally switched and I impulsively made the call to crisis. I could have saved myself, and therefore my family, an entire week of struggling had I just made that call when I first noticed what was going on inside of my brain.

Even if you are not considering inpatient, here are a few tips for in the event you do find yourself in the position I had been in.

- If you can, find a Crisis Bed Center. They are less restrictive then hospitals and can provide you with individualized care. When in crisis, that's exactly what you need. Being in a relaxed, comforting environment can heal someone much quicker and yield better results than being put in a locked ward. You can always call your local crisis line or your County's Mental Health Facility and ask them for a referral to the closest one for you.

- Have a list of questions ready. The more you ask the more you know. Some things you may want to know are:

- How long will your stay be? Mine was three to five days; however, they were willing to extend that if I felt the length of time wasn't enough. I had progressed enough that they let me go after just five days. That said, I was able to leave at any time I felt I was ready, they would not hold me there against my will.

- What should you pack? Some places do not allow you to bring anything with you. Places like this are usually very restrictive and are typically done in hospital settings. I was allowed to keep everything I brought with me except my razor. It was part of my responsibility to know if I was safe or not and it was up to me to tell staff if I felt I was unsafe or unable to contract for safety. I was thrilled that I was able to keep my journal and pen. It gave me a chance to get everything out of my head and onto paper before I went to sleep each night.

- Who can come visit you and when? This was extremely important to me. I needed to make sure that Dan and the kids would be able to visit me. I didn't want to make any promises to the kids that I couldn't keep. Thankfully they allowed my entire family to visit me unless I said otherwise. They were extremely accommodating as well. One evening Dan wasn't able to make it until after visiting hours, and they worked out a time that was good. They gave us 30 minutes together, which was quite generous of them.

- What will your day be like while you are there? I am a firm believer that those of us with bipolar disorder need structure in our lives. Knowing what I have to do and when keeps me on track. It helps me see where I am in the process of accomplishing goals I'm trying to complete. There were many people there to hold me accountable as well.

- Will you have access to a psychiatrist and are they willing to adjust any medications you may be on? Even though I have my own psychiatrist, I needed to make sure that the one I would be seeing would be willing to treat me. If he was too afraid of stepping on toes then going inpatient was going to be fruitless for me. I knew I needed a quick medication change and under the supervision of nurses and therapists this was possible.

- What type of after-care services are available to you? This is important! The last thing you want is to be thrown into the forest with a pack of wolves waiting to devour you. You need to know what you have to do after you receive inpatient care in order to remain stable. Your goal is to move past this episode and forward with your life. You don't want to find yourself having to go back into an inpatient facility soon after discharge. You may have personal issues, maybe housing issues, insurance problems, prescription coverage issues, legal problems. These are all things your case manager should be helping you with.

These are just a list of some pretty basic questions that you can ask. You may have more of your own that you can add to your list.

I'm sure by now you are wondering, *"What do I tell my children about my inpatient stay?"* I think this all depends on how much your children know about your illness. If your children are older and already know about your illness, then explaining to them that you are simply going away for a few days to get the help you need will suffice. If they are old enough to understand about your illness, then they are old enough to understand why you need this type of help. Having younger children makes the situation a little bit tougher. My younger children do not know a thing about my bipolar. They have never seen me take my medication and we rarely talk about it in front of them. This does not come from shame, but from their inability to understand something so complex. Explaining to my younger children where I was going was a bit more difficult than it was my older children. I simply told my younger children that I was going away on a trip for a few days. This was not necessarily a lie, as I was on a trip of sorts. I left out the gory details of what that trip would consist of. They were too young to understand and using terms like sick, ill, hospital, doctors, nurses can all sound scary to children who do not understand fully what you are going through. Even my 16-year-old was concerned and he was old enough to understand. My 11-year-old accepted it for what it was, but that is just the way he is. My 9-year-old on the other hand did not handle the news well at all. She had a frightening hospital stay just a month before I went inpatient and she thought where I was going would be like the place she was in. It was hard for her to understand that I was going to a different type of hospital or mental health facility than the one she was in.

Many parents ask themselves, "Do I let my children come visit me while I'm in an inpatient facility?" There are many factors at play here. How old are the children? What do they know or what can they understand about your disorder? Will the setting you are in upset or scare your children? All of these questions must be considered when allowing your children to come visit you. It would be best to know what type of setting you are going into or wait until you see the place you are going to before you promise the kids can come visit. Any pleas to come visit you can always be quelled with, *"I'll call you when I get there and let you know IF they will allow visitors."* This will give you a chance to assess the place before you decide.

In our particular case we were a little mixed about who could and who shouldn't visit. I knew for sure that I wanted Lizzie to visit. Her own hospital stay had been so traumatic for her that I needed her to see that not all mental health facilities were bad. I needed her to see that I was in a good, safe place. So she was the first to come with Dan, along with her 7-month-old sister. We did decide that it would be best for our five-year-old, our four-year-old and our 17-month-old not to visit. They are all extremely attached to me and I feared that when it was time for them to leave it would be too hard on them and ultimately hard on me as well. My 16-year-old chose not to visit. I think he was afraid of what condition I would be in. It was hard for him to understand as he isn't around all that much anyway. My 11-year-old begged to come see me, so he was also granted a visit.

Ultimately the decision is up to you and you alone. Not even your spouse or partner has a say in who you want to visit you. Going inpatient is an opportunity for you to recover and if a visitor could potentially set you back in your recovery then I would suggest not having that person visit you. Make sure you discuss this with the staff so they know which visitors are acceptable from the beginning.

Chapter Six

BEING A PARENT is the hardest job any of us has ever has to do. It doesn't matter if you are a mom or a dad or, in some cases, you find yourself being both. The job is still hard! Add bipolar to the mix and now your challenges have gotten a lot harder. But, just because they are harder, doesn't mean they can't be overcome. I'd like to believe the first place to start is prioritizing. Easy, right? Well, if you are anything like me the answer is no. Prioritizing is one of the most difficult things for me to do. I always think everything needs to be done RIGHT NOW! It can't wait and needs to be done immediately. I like instant gratification. In the real world, it just doesn't work that way. Bipolar parents must prioritize or else we will find ourselves in a heap of trouble. If we don't take steps to pare our endless lists down, we are setting ourselves up for disaster. Things work different for us; not worse, just different and we need to learn to live within our bipolar means. So how do we actually go about doing this? I wish I could say I had it all figured out, but I don't. What I can offer you is a little of what I learned along the way. Let's start with the obvious.

- Take care of yourself first! I know this sounds extremely selfish, but you really do need to put yourself first. There is a huge difference between being selfish and doing self-care. Selfishness is the act of caring for one's own desires without concern for others. Self-care is making sure you are improving yourself so you can care for the ones around you. These are two very different things.

- Spend time with your children. Listen, the dust bunnies, the dishes, the laundry....it'll always be there. No sooner will you clean up and some mysterious pile will show up in the spot you just cleaned. Your children, however, will one day grow up and move out, possibly far away. Spending time with your children will also be therapeutic for you. It's a chance to relax and just have some fun. I love to color, and it's the one thing my kids and I love to do together. There's nothing more satisfying to me than playing with my kids.

- Take it day by day. Small baby steps. Just putting one foot in front of the other is all it takes. When you are in the midst of an episode or a med change, it may seem like everything you do is overwhelming and insurmountable and, at times, everything is. All you can do is try. When you are feeling better, try harder.

- Know when to say, *"NO!"* This means even to your immediate family members. My oldest son loves to come walking out of his bedroom and request a ride to somewhere, or to announce that he and girlfriend want to get together that particular day. I always say "No!" Why.... because I need warning. I need time to collect myself and if I'm feeling unwell, then there is no way I want company, even if she's not there to see me. That said, I do not say no to doctor appointments, therapy appointments, school functions, etc.

- Make a list! Not a big one, not even a medium one, but a small one; just a list of a few things that you need or want to get done. It could include simple things like shower, brush your teeth, do one load of laundry, wash dishes, spend the rest of the day with the kids, go for a walk, watch a movie with your spouse or partner. Sometimes you may find that just showering is enough and you spend the rest of the day lounging on the couch, watching cartoons with your kids. THAT'S OKAY! Other days you may find that you accomplish what you need to in a very short amount of time, and you feel well enough to do more. Feel free to add in a few small things, but don't overdo it.

- Be gentle with yourself and remember the first one, TAKE CARE OF YOU! Taking care of yourself should be your first priority. If you are not well, you will not be able to take care of anyone else. I understand all too well what it is like to get bogged down by daily life and how easy it is to forget that I am supposed to be taking care of me first. With seven children, a husband and a dog, you can see how easy it would be for me to forget. I have to keep on top of myself. Sometimes that means letting go of the housework and passing it off to someone else in the house to take care of.

There have been times when I have found myself alone and with no one to turn to for help. For many of us, we are unable to work. As a result, the other adult in the home must go to work and provide the income. Sometimes we find ourselves without any friends or family to pitch in when we need them to. I have found myself in this situation more than once and it's a very unpleasant place to be. Unfortunately, it's during these times that we have to put our rain gear on and weather the storm by ourselves. But there is help out there; we just have to find it within ourselves to look for it.

For a long time I internalized everything I had been feeling. I did this because I didn't want my children to see the ugly side of me. Going it alone and internalizing everything is what sent me into the horrid mixed episode I went through back in 2011. It wasn't until I started reaching out to others for help that I received any type of relief. This meant me swallowing my pride a lot and it also meant me pushing through my social anxieties and allowing people into my home and my life so I could receive some kind of support. A lot of us fear reaching out to others. We worry we will be judged or condemned, or worse, institutionalized for the way we feel or think. But if we find trusted individuals who understand our disorder we can find some sort of peace during and after our recovery time. If a friend or family member offers to take the kids for the day, don't feel bad or worry about burdening them, they are offering and you should take them up on that offer. In my experience, if you continue to turn down offers, then those offers stop coming and you soon find yourself in a position where you have to ask. If you are anything like me, I hate asking for help. To me it shows that I am weak and I can no longer do this alone.

Don't worry if you have to ask, though. This does not mean you are weak, it means you are strong and you know your limitations before you become weak. Asking for help is a sign of strength, not weakness. If you have a trusted family member or friend, but that person doesn't know about your illness and you aren't ready to tell him or her, don't worry. You only have to give out as much information as you are comfortable with, and saying you don't feel well is not telling a lie. I learned a lot of this the hard way. My refusal to accept or ask for help is what turned me into being a crappy mom for a while. I was too stubborn to face the truth and realize I couldn't do my job anymore. Had I swallowed my pride, admitted where I went wrong and asked or reached out to those that I trusted, I would have recovered quicker.

Sometimes people don't offer their help because they are afraid they will make you feel uncomfortable. They may think that by them offering, you may believe they don't think you can do your job. This is far from the truth. Offers to help you are just that, they want to help you and you should let them. You deserve to get better or to take the break that you need so you don't end up symptomatic. Having someone take your kids for an afternoon or even for a few days as an attempt to avoid an episode shows that you are being responsible. It shows that you know your limitations, and it shows that you are an awesome parent! But what happens when you find yourself with no one? Who do you turn to when there are no more offers, or people say no, or your spouse has no more sick time or vacation time, or you're a single parent with no one to turn to? There are still people who want to help you, and there are still ways to get support from others. If you belong to a church, reach out to them. Again, you don't need to be specific about your illness; no one needs to know details. All they need to know is you are not feeling well and you need some help. If you have a Salvation Army or United Way, many of them can offer support of some kind as well. Sometimes it may only be in the form of food, clothing or a financial donation, but any stress you don't have to worry about is a good thing. Avoiding anything that could trigger an episode is important. There are many older adults who have no children or grandchildren, and they would be willing to pitch in as well.

I have found that if you can spare the extra dollars, hiring a high school student who can come and take the kids for a few hours can be of much help. Kids love playing with kids and if that high school kid is someone you know and can trust, then by all means take advantage of that kind of help. Become a member of your local Nami or DBSA, as they will be of some assistance to you as well. They could be invaluable when it comes to resources and may be able to direct you to other organizations in your area that you are unaware of. No help from anyone can be the most difficult thing a mentally ill parent must face and it can sometimes be the one reason we reach the ending point where we feel hopeless.

I remember a few weeks between the months of May 2011 until about July 2011 where I spent most of my time lounging on the couch, with my young children using our living room as their own personal play space. I put up baby gates and child-proofed everything. I let them watch way too much TV, did no potty training with anyone, and only did the basics, which weren't much. Many nights Dan had to do the dinner and cleanup, and if dinner was up to me because he had to work late, the kids ate cereal or microwavable meals. I did the best I could under the circumstances, and I don't feel guilty for it. Normal me, stable me, is NOT that person, but depressed me is, and depression is not something I or any of us can control. We can manage it with medication and therapy, but sometimes, we may still find ourselves completely and totally spent and in need of some necessary help. I have not always used the resources available to me, but I have made a promise to myself that next time I will. My family's lives need to go on even if mine is in a disaster. My children need to know they have someone to count on when I'm not feeling the best. It's no different than if you had the flu, or worse. Everyone needs help and no one should be ashamed to ask for that help. Sometimes, those we reach out to, those that become a part of our support network, those that end up being more understanding, become part of our family in a way we never imagined was possible.

As you can see, finding balance in our bipolar world is almost impossible. No sooner are we feeling well, and we are slipping again. There have been many times I have beaten myself up because I wasn't well enough to care for my children. It took episode after episode and lots of outreach from my friends in order for me to realize that there were parts of my illness that I could not control. Guilt is a horrible thing and it's something that attaches itself to us during symptomatic times. I often feel guilty about not being the mom I know I am when I'm well. Throughout depressive episodes, I find myself wondering how my children are handling all this, what they must think of me, how they must hate me, and the list goes on. One thing that sticks out the most, whether I'm ill or not, is how are my children coping? It would be nice if we didn't have to even consider that, but we do.

It's our first responsibility to make sure our illness doesn't affect our children's everyday lives. Sure, there are going to be moments where you will have to say no to a certain activity because you know that doing that activity is not good for your mental health. You may be having a hard day and not feeling up to a play date with a bunch of 10-year-old girls, there's nothing wrong with that. Even parents who do not have a mental illness say no when they are not feeling up to something like this. It is when our illness affects our children's education or our children's social lives, or affects the family as a whole that we must step back and see where we need help the most. If we find ourselves overwhelmed by constantly running our children from activity to activity, keeping up with the housework, getting all the laundry done and frantically staying on top of homework, then we crash into debilitating depression. Or, we become too irritable because of a manic episode. Worse, we become aggressive because we are mixed. When that happens, then our illness is absolutely affecting our children's lives. It is before all of this happens that we must have a plan in place, one that protects our children.

The one hard truth is our illness does have an impact on our children's lives when we are symptomatic, and we must find a way to help them to cope when we can't cope ourselves. I think a lot of this will depend on how much support you have, and who can you turn to in the event that you find yourself in crisis. Just like all parents get the flu, bipolar parents get sick as well. It would be beneficial to have someone who can either come in and help with the kids or better yet, take the kids until you start feeling better. No child should have to see what their parents are going through when they are in the midst of an episode, especially our mixed or depressive times.

Helping children to understand that your illness is not because of them is extremely important. When children can't see what the illness is, it's hard for them to comprehend it. When Mommy or Daddy is in the bathroom throwing up, they understand that we have the stomach flu and are sick. If they see us crying all day, they may think it's something they have done to upset you. If you are running around, non-stop, hyperactive and yelling at them for getting in your way, they may feel sad because they were just trying to help you clean up or trying to play in an area you were trying to run around in. They may not understand the sudden changes in you, and may attribute a lot of your behavior to their own behaviors. If you are lying around on the couch, depressed out of your mind, but screaming at them for everything they are doing, they are certainly going to feel guilty for how you keep responding to them. Keeping yourself in check, keeping yourself grounded is one way you can help your children. Before you start yelling at them, take a moment to think if what you are yelling at would bother you on a "normal" day. Sometimes, just taking a five or ten minute break outside, breathing deeply for a few moments, can make all the difference in the world. I find myself constantly checking myself against reality. When my kids are acting up or just being kids and playing, making messes like kids do and I feel the urgency coming on to yell at them, I have learned to spin on my heel and walk the other way. I go into the bathroom or outside for a few minutes to catch my breath and think about how I want to handle the situation. When I am depressed, I try very hard to replace all those repetitive thoughts of, can't, shouldn't, wouldn't, and couldn't with words like can, should, would, and could. I remind myself that I am a good mom and I can do this.

If you can keep track of yourself and your moods then you are helping your children. Knowing your limitations and the difference between a little bit mad and out of your mind full of rage, you can stop yourself and collect yourself before you fly off the handle. If it's depression that's causing you difficulty, again, start replacing those negative thoughts. Even if you don't want to, spend 10 or 15 minutes cuddling with your children, coloring with them or rolling around on the floor. I promise you, in that 15 minutes you will feel better about yourself and you will have shown your children that you love them and care about them. Learn about yourself. Learn your limitations, your triggers, how much you can do comfortably without the stress building up to the point that you come crashing down in true bipolar fashion. Find the tools that help you the most. A few things that help me when I'm entering an episode is to try and get it under control with a call to my psychiatrist. Sometimes all it takes is a medication tweak. In my honest opinion, 90% of our disorder can be managed with medication, but we do have to pull our own weight. Saying we can't control our emotions or we can't manage our illness shows that we are weak and we are not willing to give it our all. We must give it our all for our children's sake.

- Try a medication tweak first.

- Try to get some outside help until you feel better.

- If no outside help is available, try to find some tools to help you cope. Breathing exercises, relaxation techniques, journaling and taking a break are just a few examples. If you are coping, then so are your children. There are times when we have to push through and brave the storm alone. Having your rain gear in check will help you through these times.

- Learn your limitations.

- If your children are old enough, explain your disorder to them. This will help them understand that your episodes have absolutely nothing to do with them. They will forgive you if they know more about your disorder.

- Forgive yourself and move on. There is no sense in beating yourself up. Learn your lesson and then find ways to go into combat next time knowing you will be able to overcome this.

Depression is the only thing that I know of that goes against gravity. There is always a way up, and for parents that way is usually through or because of our children. We must trudge on because they need to have us at our best. Try to be gentle with yourself and especially your children. Don't be too hard on them. Your illness is not their problem. It is yours and you have to take every step to ensure that they are not terribly affected by it. Recovery is what I strive for, but I must first get and remain stable. Once I am, I know recovery is right around the corner for me. It's just a matter of getting over that last, little mountain that seems so monumental at the moment. Whether you are manic or you are depressed, these are all steps you can take to protect your children from the gory side of our illness. When I was first diagnosed, I thought it was the best thing to walk in the door and announce that Mommy had bipolar and that was what was wrong with her. I'm glad my adult brain kicked in and realized that this was probably not a good idea. My oldest knew I had a doctor's appointment and he was fully aware of what had happened to lead to this appointment. He knew what kind of doctor I was going to see, so naturally he wanted to know and I told him. I don't think he fully understands it, but he knows I'm moody, he knows I get stressed easily and he knows that I cry like there is no tomorrow sometimes. He also knows that I can scream, a lot, over the smallest things. Danny also knows that I take medications to try and control these symptoms and he knows that sometimes these medications don't always work. That said, he knows enough about my illness that our arguments have gotten less and less. This is most likely a combination of him knowing my issues were never because of or about him, and me taking my medications and getting proper treatment.

My younger children, however, had no clue what was going on with me. That is until one morning Andrew came across the booklet the psychiatrist gave me about bipolar disorder. It was then the questions began and unfortunately those questions were asked in front of Lizzie, who then had questions of her own. Their main ones were, *"What is bipolar?"*... ..."*Are you sick?"*....."*Is this what you have?"* Answering their questions was not by any means easy. How do you explain something so complex to your children without scaring the living daylights out of them? I was honest, though, and I told them, *"Yes, Mommy does have bipolar, but I take medication now to help control it."* I explained a lot about how bipolar affected me and my moods, but they seemed more confused by my explanations. So, I asked for a little more time to think about how to explain it so they would best understand it. Thankfully they understood and their pressing questions stopped. That particular day was sunny and warm, and there was a small rain shower that left a rainbow in the sky.....soon the clouds rolled in along with the thunder and the wind. Lightening was flashing. It was then that it hit me how to explain my illness to my children. So I called them back out to the kitchen and this is what I told them.

"Mommy is not sick, but her brain is. I do take medication to make it better. Sometimes the medication works and sometimes it doesn't. Bipolar works very much like the weather." They both sat there, waiting for me to go on as they still did not understand what I was trying to tell them, so I went on. *"This morning, the sun was shining and sometimes Mommy's brain is smiling too, sometimes that sunshine is so bright that I want to run and play and soak up as much of it as I can."* Now I had their attention! *"Later today, the weather changed and it was all dark and cloudy. Sometimes Mommy's brain is like that, too. Like a thick, black thunder-cloud just waiting to burst and when it does, it's like the wind. In plain words, sometimes Mommy's brain is full of sunshine and rainbows. Other times it's like a thunderstorm with a hurricane and a tornado mixed together."* They sat thinking, letting all this new information sink in. Andrew was the first one to understand. He's completely obsessed with the weather, especially those storm chaser shows. Once he understood and began babbling about it, Lizzie understood, too. I think they both view it in terms like Danny does and it's enough for them to understand for now. I'm sure this explanation has helped Lizzie better understand her own illness as well. I think a lot of how or maybe the question should be addressed when you explain your illness to your children depends on how old your children are and if you are comfortable speaking to them about it. How much of it would they understand? If they aren't asking questions, should you

even strike up a conversation about it with them? I also needed to explain to my children that although having bipolar disorder is not something to be ashamed of, many people don't understand it and therefore it scares them. I asked them to please keep this information to themselves. The last thing you want is your child parading around school singing, "*My mom/dad has bipolar disorder!*"

Many children do not understand mental illness. If you tried to explain the stigma that surrounds the mental health community, you'd probably end up sparking more fear then actually helping them understand. There are many people becoming more receptive to the idea that mental illness truly exists and those suffering need help. Kids, however, are a different story. Many have only heard horror stories about someone with bipolar or schizophrenia. They do not understand it fully and so the bullying and teasing begin. I gave my children this answer as to why I didn't want them talking about it to their friends or teachers.

"*Although I am not ashamed or embarrassed by having bipolar, some of your friends would most likely be uncomfortable knowing this information. A lot of people are afraid of something because they don't understand it. It would be a good idea to not talk about this with anyone for a while.*" They seemed satisfied with that statement and I really don't know if they ever discussed it with anyone. If they have, there have never been any ramifications because of it. I do know that Danny's girlfriend and her parents are aware of my illness, and I'm thankful that they've never held any contempt towards us because of it. Having them know has actually been of benefit for us, as they are willing to pitch in and help when we've needed them to. They've been supportive and caring towards Danny.

We have not discussed this with any of our children under the age of five. Josh is just a five-year-old and I do not think any child of that age or younger is capable of understanding, even with the weather explanation. It is just too big and too complex for their little minds to hold onto. I'm also a firm believer in, *"If they are old enough to ask, then they are old enough to know."* So far, we have not crossed that bridge, but I know a time will come when they will either see me taking my medications, or I will end up inpatient when they are older. I would prefer to have them know and understand before an inpatient stay was necessary, as that could lead to less than desirable reactions from both of them.

Chapter Seven

I PERSONALLY DON'T HAVE many people to turn to in the event that I find myself in a crisis situation. I have my husband and a handful of friends whom I can turn to when times get tough. Outside of them, there are very few family members I have left. The ones who are left either live clear across the country, or throughout the years have severed any relationships with me. Sometimes I have been the one doing the severing. I have learned toxic people bring you down. Misery loves company, and as a bipolar parent who is trying to do her best to remain stable, people like that have no place in my life.

There was a time when I had one of the biggest supporters in the world. No, I'm not talking financial support here, I'm talking emotionally. That person was there for me no matter what, no matter what time of the day or night it was. She was the one person I could count on in any situation, the one person I knew I could trust to watch my children, and she did this often at the drop of a hat. This person never cast judgment upon me or my children's behavior. She knew how to approach sensitive situations with me, and she would typically be thoughtful when it came to discussing matters that may upset me. She usually knew just the right words to use to keep me grounded and in check. She knew me better than anyone else in the entire world, probably better then Dan even knew me at the time. We had our moments, times when we did not see eye to eye. Times we would argue or have a fight that resulted in a few days of not speaking to each other, but never more than a few days. She was always supportive and encouraging even when she didn't agree with some choice we may have been making at the time.

That person was ripped from our lives in November of 2006, just five weeks after the birth of Joshua. Having so many children was not an area she supported and she would tell us how concerned she was for us. She worried about finances and our ability to take care of our children. In that respect she was correct. But as each child was born, she was as much in love with that baby as she had been the first. She loved her grandchildren in a way that no other family member has ever loved my children or me alone. She adored Dan and would constantly remark about how lucky I was. She helped me to see that even when things looked cloudy and grey and I wasn't able to see it for myself.

Losing my mom was like losing the life-line to my entire existence. Very soon after her death, family members who were once there for me, if only to chat on the phone, drifted away. I was terribly depressed, alone in my grief, and a psychiatrist at our County Mental Health facility prescribed me Prozac and Trazodone. I was only being treated for the situational depression. No one had figured out that I had bipolar at this time. That was six years ago. This combination of medication sent me into a frenzied manic episode. My judgment was off and I was unable to make good decisions for myself, let alone for my family. This truly was one of the craziest manic episodes of my life. I pushed my family into believing we had to move, and we had to move now. Within three weeks we had the entire house packed up, a U-Haul rented and we were off to North Carolina. I have no idea what I was thinking, but I was not in my right mind. I even convinced Dan it was a good idea to sign our home over to the bank, that we needed a fresh start and this was the way to go. Dan had no job waiting for him in North Carolina, but I was hoping to create a relationship with his family. When this didn't work out, we packed it up and made another impulsive move to Utah to be near my brother. Here I must give my brother some credit. I was "sick" but no one knew it and no one knew what it was like to be in my batshit, crazy head. But he moved me, Dan and our four children into his home in an attempt to help us. I will be forever thankful to him for his generosity and for putting up with me and my not-so-perfect children. Except there was one problem. We didn't have a place of our own to live and I was not very good with living with someone else, nor was I good with handling money. Being manic, I spent the money Dan was making quicker than he could bring it home. I refused to get a job because I didn't want to inconvenience my sister-in-law with my four children, and I knew no one who could watch them. We also couldn't afford daycare. If at that time I would have been able to recognize my symptoms, if we had known that spending money as much as I did was a huge problem for me, if I could have just swallowed my pride and asked my brother to hold a certain amount of Dan's pay, we could have had a place of our own. But we didn't know and I was terribly embarrassed to admit that we just didn't have the money to move out.

After I learned I was pregnant again, I was humiliated. Not because I was pregnant, but because I was there, living under my brother's roof, no money to my name, four children already and pregnant again. I decided again, impulsively, to move back home to Pennsylvania. No one wanted to go. Everyone voted against it, even Dan. He had a job he enjoyed, the kids loved the schools and had made friends. We would spend hours playing in my brother's backyard. I knew the kids would miss all of those things, but I insisted. I cried because I had crashed and was depressed, and I needed to go somewhere else besides where I was. I wanted to go home. I wanted my life back. I wanted to be in my own home, and I wanted to feel "normal" again. When I said I needed help and no one in Utah could help me, I will never forget my sister-in-law's words to me, *"Well, why can't we help you?"* My only answer was blunt....."*Because you have full-time jobs, you can't help me. I need to be around people who can. I want to go back to my old doctors. I want to go home."*

Thing is, that really wasn't the truth. I didn't really want to go, but I didn't know what I wanted. I was making bad decision after bad decision and I didn't know what the right thing to do was. I needed my family's help, but I didn't know how to ask for it. I needed more than financial help. I needed emotional support, and this was something I didn't think my family could give me. I wasn't willing to admit to my faults, that I had no money to move out, that I had squandered everything Dan and I had, that I had been stupid and foolish and that I was Out. Of. My. Mind. Crazy! I thought if I ran from the crazies and tucked my tail between my legs things would get better. Instead, I should have swallowed my pride and been honest, because where Dan, the kids and I sit now is worse off than when we were in Utah.

The problem with bipolar disorder; we never see our mistakes until after the fact. We are prone to making bad decisions, and that's why it's best to not make any decisions when we are symptomatic. It is one thing that no family should have to deal with, one that no one should take on without getting therapy for themselves and being as educated as possible about the disorder. Whether it's for yourself or for a loved one....it's the best thing you can do to maintain the family relationships we all so desperately need.

In marriages where one spouse is diagnosed with bipolar disorder, 90% of the time those marriages end in divorce. Both partners are to blame for this, as no marriage ends because of just one person. Both partners must do their part in order for any marriage to succeed. It's hard work, no one will tell you that when you get married. Marriage is not 50/50. If you aren't doing 100% yourself, then you shouldn't be expecting 100% from your significant other. If you are only doing 50% of the work, then that's all your partner should be expected to give and in any marriage, regardless of the circumstances, 50% is not enough. When bipolar is thrown into the mix, or any mental illness for that matter, the job becomes almost impossible. Almost impossible sounds pretty terrible, but it's really not. Anything is possible if we are giving it our all. My husband and I have been together since 1993. For many, many years, I went wrongly diagnosed as having major depressive disorder and any and all medications sent me either manic or into an irritable, aggressive mixed state. But Dan stood by my side, through all the good and all the bad, and he's still here with me today. When someone truly loves another person, they are able to look past their faults and see the true person underneath it all.

The best advice I can give you is to hold on to hope. Hold on to it with everything you have. Without hope, all else will fail. When you have nothing to hang on to....there is truly nothing left and that even applies to marriage. Sure, you may be able to start over, but will you be able to do that without wondering if you could have helped the one you love, much more than you had. Or if you are the bipolar spouse, you may always wonder what you had done wrong or how you could have changed in order to save your marriage. I believe change is possible, if you want it enough. Bipolar diagnoses aren't just for the individual spouse, but for the family as a whole. For there is no pebble thrown into a pond that doesn't cause the water to ripple, commonly known as the ripple effect. There is no doubt that your diagnosis will affect you, your spouse and your children. It is your responsibility as a couple to learn how to manage this illness together. I suggest individual therapy, along with some couple's therapy. This will provide you a safe haven to get off your chest what you need to about each other. It will also give you both the opportunity to learn how to manage this illness together. There are many reasons bipolar marriages end in divorce.

Here are just a few:

- Reckless Behavior - spending sprees, infidelity, driving while intoxicated or on drugs, partying.

- Substance Abuse

- Financial Burden

- Inability to remain employed for long periods of time.

All of the reasons listed above can be managed with proper treatment from his or her psychiatrist and treatment team. Working with a good therapist that is knowledgeable in bipolar disorder can help you learn how to manage those things when you are symptomatic. There are many coping skills that can be utilized so you can overcome the problems listed above. You must have the willingness to do everything in your power to get better and remain well for as long as you can. You can do this quicker and easier with the help of your spouse or partner. So, how does a partner help a bipolar spouse? It's not simple and it's not easy and it's not for the cowardly. Understanding is a key factor. Someone living with bipolar cannot just snap out of it, and telling one to do so is both ignorant and condescending. Bipolar people have a very hard time controlling their emotions, and during episodes, their actions as well. They need to know that they can count on you when things have gone funky. A casual comment or joke that when under stable circumstances would seem okay can cause a very much undesired reaction from your bipolar spouse when they are not stable. You may find them depressed or agitated because of something that appeared to you as innocent fun. Try not to make a big deal out of this. Trying to state your point will most likely spark an argument that could have been avoided.

Mild criticisms can bring on thoughts of suicide. The bipolar spouse may view these criticisms as put-downs, or may reiterate what their brains are trying to say to them. When I'm depressed, I often have voices telling me that I'm worthless and that my family would be better off without me. Making small remarks about your spouse's appearance or how they are functioning could send them off into a suicidal depression. If there is something that your bipolar spouse has done to upset you, you need to choose your words carefully and approach the situation with sensitivity and compassion. A bipolar marriage is stressful, to say the least. It is typically full of misunderstandings and conflicts. That's why I stress couple's therapy so much. Having an objective point of view from an experienced counselor can help both partners learn how to team together instead of raging a war against one another. The healthy spouse plays an important role in a successful bipolar marriage. This is because if treatment and management of your spouse is not under control, it's going to be up to you to make sure things are running smoothly. This is especially important when you have children involved.

During an episode, the last thing you want to do is add on stress by criticizing your spouse for not getting out of bed and sleeping all day. Or maybe your spouse finds themselves right smack in the middle of a manic spending spree and depletes your entire savings that you may have had saved to move into a new home. Those things are fixable, even if they don't seem so at the time. Guilt and shame are the last things a depressed or manic person should have to feel as we sometimes tend to act impulsively. It may be up to you to reach out to others to find the help your spouse needs so you can go to work and continue bringing home an income. Knowing the house is clean and your children are cared for can take a lot of stress off of each other during symptomatic times. The most important thing a spouse can do for their bipolar partner is to offer them understanding and support. Encourage them to take their medication and to work with their treatment team. Gentle reminders that things will get better are always good, too. One must be patient with the bipolar spouse and not expect them to recover quickly from any episode, whether it be depression, manic or mixed. Recovery takes a long time and sometimes can stretch into months or possibly years if treatment isn't quite right yet. The more support they have from you and their treatment team, the faster recovery will take place. Remembering that it may be a long time before your spouse is able to function at a level you are used to or one you think is normal is beneficial as well.

A spouse can watch for signs indicating that an episode may be on the horizon and can take appropriate steps to try and curb or at the very least lessen the impact for both parties involved. Being prepared is an invaluable tool. The couple should sit down together and discuss possible triggers that can send one either manic, depressed or both. Having such a plan in place can sometimes stop any damage from being done. This might include moving money from your joint checking into a private savings account. Remove alcohol and other substances from the home. Maybe hiding the car keys if your spouse becomes intoxicated or high. Taking control of their medications and at worst, having your spouse hospitalized if they are threatening to harm themselves or others.

Any suicidal thoughts, remarks or actions should be taken seriously and reported immediately to your spouse's treatment team. This is not something to take as an idle threat. It is a call for help and it is your responsibility to insure your spouse gets the help she or he needs. Emotional support, encouragement, reminders of how much your spouse is loved and cared for can be of tremendous help. What both partners need to understand is, there isn't just a marriage you are trying to save, but a person - the person you fell in love with, the person you vowed you could never live without. Remember, hold on to hope! Like all marriages, Dan and I have had our ups and downs. Unfortunately, I have to say we've had more downs than ups in the last 19 years.

Having bipolar disorder has done three things for our marriage. It has ended up in raging, explosive arguments. These are the times I regret the most, but they are also the times I've learned the most from. These types of arguments have taught me just how much I've needed to learn self-control. They have forced me to take a critical look at myself and change the behaviors that instigate these kinds of arguments. No one wants to be verbally abused and in my case, being the verbal abuser, I have humiliated myself on more than one occasion. It's during these times, that Dan had every right to kick me to the curb. Instead, he kept on loving me, because he could see my "normal" periods, my stable times and it was that person he loved and knew he would always get back.

Bipolar has also built a wall around me that at times, is quite hard to break down. Especially when I'm depressed, I feel vulnerable and unable to speak the emotions and words that I need to convey to him at the time. It usually takes lots of coaxing or me finding the nerve to write out how I'm feeling in a letter to him. Sometimes the latter is the best way. Due to the way my brain is working, but the words just won't come out of my mouth in the manner that my brain is trying to present them. Putting my emotions and thoughts out on paper also helps to get these thoughts out of my head.

There have been some good things that have come from the illness I suffer from. During manic times, I tend to be much more vocal about how much I truly love my husband. I'm also touchy, feely and love to hug and kiss him, shower him with my love and do just about everything I can to let him know he is the only one I want to be with in my life. It's during these times that I'm more able to show my appreciation for him. When I'm manic, my complete being is much lighter and we can joke and laugh at just about anything together. It has also produced some of the best sex ever. I guess this would explain why we have seven children!

On the flip side of this, I can still remember the first time I ever had a raging fit on Dan. We were fighting, I was tired, working a full time job, he was working afternoons and we both weren't cut out for this job of living on our own yet. Danny was just about seven months old and tension between the two of us was high. I remember being so agitated with Dan, the first thing I thought to do was grab a knife, not because he was threatening me, but because I did not know what to do with my anger. We struggled for a while, him trying to get the knife away without getting hurt and me struggling to keep my hold on the knife. Eventually he won, thank God. I would hate to think of what I could have done to him or myself had he not gotten a hold of it. I was out of my mind and I don't know if I would have actually hurt him or not. The crazies had gotten a hold of me in a way that I'll never forget. In either case, he saved not only his own life, but mine as well. That incident made me lose more than I ever thought I would. Three days later, Dan hopped on a bus and took off. He left Danny with my mother while I was working and went to be with his family for a while. He needed time to figure out what was the right thing to do. He needed time to clear his head and to figure out if coming back to me was even worth it anymore. I used to blame him, but in this case, I have to take my 100% and admit I was in the wrong. He did the only logical thing there was to do at the time.

Dan leaving left me broken and lost. For the first time since I was 15 years old, I was contemplating suicide. I had lost my only support person, my best friend, and I didn't think I could go on in life without him. I cried until I was completely dry and then had my mother's fiancé drive me to the hospital. The caseworker explained that if I admitted myself it would be a 10-day-stay and I wouldn't be allowed any visitors. I refused. I believe this is what led me to beg the hospital not to admit me when I had my first breakdown. I couldn't imagine going ten days without any contact from friends or family, especially Dan or my children. There have been many times through the years that I've often wondered why Dan came back. One day I actually got up the courage to ask him. His response was quite overwhelming at the time as I was in a deep, dark, suicidal depression. His answer, *"Because I always knew there was a good you underneath it all. That you weren't that kind of person and you'd get better."* I believe those words are what kept me fighting for my life.

I have been far from the best wife in the world. I definitely will not EVER win that award. Dan has had so many opportunities to just up and leave, walk out and never look back. So many reasons why he should do exactly that. So many reasons why he should kick me to the curb and lock the door behind me. Other than that first time, he never has. No, I will not win any awards, but he surely should. He's amazing and understanding and extremely supportive of whatever I am going through. He's had his share of my aggression, verbal and physical abuse, depression that left him having to work full-time and deal with everything else at home. Me being angry when I didn't understand why he couldn't keep up with my manic times, hyper-sexuality, substance and alcohol abuse. And now he has to deal with me being on a medication merry-go-round that has caused some ridiculous side effects. Times of me being non-functional due to over-medication and medications just plain and simply not working. The entire time he has stood by me. He's been there even when he had every right NOT to be there. I do not know what it is, maybe the power of love is much more than I could ever imagine. A power I have yet to grasp a hold of myself. I doubt I would love me as much as he has. It's an odd combination, bipolar and love. One that I don't think many of us think is achievable. We allow our diagnoses to define us in such a way that we feel unworthy of any kind of love. But it really doesn't have to be that way. I promise you that.

May 22, 1999, Dan and I said those famous words, *"In sickness and in health."* I don't think either of us knew exactly how literal or immediate that would be. I'm sure we both thought about it in the long-term. When we were both old and feeble. When we needed to rely on the other one for support and comfort. Maybe during things like the flu or a cold or maybe worse. But I know we never imagined it would come down to mental sickness. I don't think it would have made any difference to Dan if he had known then what we both know now. After all, he did come back after that one aggressive moment. I have learned a few things about Bipolar and Love. If you are with a loving, supportive spouse, your love for one another can blossom during and after times of difficulty. Forgiveness breeds something mystical, something none of us can understand. When a couple has come to a place where they can forgive and still love...it's an amazing feeling. But it wasn't always that way. There were often times I felt lonely and sad - trapped within my own head, my own thoughts and my own emotions. I was afraid that if I let even my husband know what was going on in there, he would have me committed to the loony bin, and by all the rights. I was positive of it, so for years I suffered in silence. That silence built a wall between us, communication started to break down and our marriage was soon in trouble for reasons that neither of us understood. Soon we weren't even in the same book, let alone the same page. The issue with this, I was so far deep into myself, I couldn't even recognize it and didn't understand when things began falling apart. Within time, we were able to start picking up the pieces. One by one, we'd examine it and find the proper place that it fit into. Much the same as putting together a puzzle. There were many moments throughout this that I know I dropped my piece. It got lost somewhere among the other millions of small pieces that were gathered in a pile on the floor and it was up to me to have to get on my knees, digging around looking for that piece. There were times, admittedly, that I didn't want to. It was those times that even though I felt I was unworthy of love, Dan still loved me, and you know what? He got down there and helped me search for the piece that was missing. We'd find it, place it together and it would fit perfectly.

I learned throughout the years that when I was at my worst, I could take advantage of the love, kindness and patience that had been dished out to me in heaping mounds. That was part of why the wall was built, why the communication broke down. I was unwilling to give any information even though Dan was willing to give all of himself to me. I learned that I was the selfish spouse and was not giving back, helping him to understand why I was the way I was. Maybe it's because I didn't know why at the time. But once I learned, I began to give it up, even if in just small ways.

One of the greatest lessons I learned was, I can give love even when I'm feeling at my worst. Sometimes this is better than any medication or therapy or relaxation technique I could learn. Just the act of wrapping my arms around the man I love and accepting his love in return is enough to make it all okay. Even if it's just a few moments in time. Love is about how much you give, not about how much you get. I do not do well at dishing it out, hell, I'm not even good at receiving it. But I try. I forgive myself and I forgive Dan and I pick myself up and try to do it again. Because that to me is what a marriage is about. Trying, giving and trying some more when you are able and forgiving the rest.

Chapter Eight

THE NEGATIVE EFFECTS bipolar has had on my marriage have equally if not more so affected my children. Back before I was being treated, I didn't realize the hell my children went through. One day, Mommy was all sunshine and rainbows. Playing games, brushing off the mess the kiddos had made, making dinner, running around with them. The house was organized and clean. I didn't mind their never-ending questions and always answered them with patience. The next day, I was biting their heads off, yapping at them for getting crumbs on my freshly shampooed carpets, complaining about getting no help from anyone. I was refusing to play because I now had to clean up everyone's messes. The next day they'd see Mom, lounging on the couch, oblivious to anything going on around her, the kids using the living room as one big playpen. They watched a little too much TV and Mommy would hand them snack cakes for lunch because she was too exhausted to do anything else. Dinner was mostly a fend-for-yourself event and if you couldn't fend, then you'd have to wait for Daddy. None of the states I was in was good for my children. It caused confusion and fear in every one of them. They had no consistency, no idea what to expect. Everyone walked on eggshells around me; no one trusted what mood I might be in.

After receiving the proper treatment, things did get better, for a while. The kids knew they could count on me to answer their questions with patience, the house was clean, but no compulsively so. I didn't snap when crumbs were everywhere. I simply vacuumed them up or waited till the end of the day when no one else was going to make any more crumbs. I would play with my children, laugh with my children and for a while, I was just Mommy and it felt good. Things were getting done, but not to the point of over-productivity. It felt....strange to feel so normal and I could tell it felt strange to my kids as well. They were always waiting on edge for when the other shoe would drop. When would Mommy's moods change and when would they start getting yelled at again or worse, when would Mommy crash to the couch and not care about herself, let alone anyone around her. I wish I could say that things remained stable. But the truth is they didn't. If you remember, things began to slide back downhill and quite fast. My children along with myself sit on edge every day just waiting for the polar shift. My children, I think....have learned how to deal with it. They know it's not them, they know it's me. Is any of that fair to them? Absolutely not and I long for the day when they could say, my Mom has been well for x amount of years. Not just weeks, not just months. My children want and absolutely deserve for me to be recovered, in remission. The younger children have no idea how to cope or what to expect. When will Mommy be Mommy again? They know it's coming and it's something their small brains do not understand. An eye opener for me was when one afternoon I plopped down on the couch next to Joshy. Instead of him cuddling close to me....he moved to the other end of the couch. At first I was hurt. Why would he do that? I had been fine with him and his siblings lately. Why would he move away from me? I was heartbroken. The more I thought about it, the more I realized he was just responding to what he's used to. For ten months it had been such hell for him that the only time Mommy plopped next to him was to either ask him to move so I could lay down or to snap at him. He wanted nothing to do with either of those things and I don't blame him.

For reasons I still have yet to understand, why has Joshy taken the brunt of my illness? I don't know if it's because when he was born, there was a limited amount of time I to bond with him. The bipolar was in full swing by then. For whatever reason, I knew I needed to find a way to correct this problem. I do not do well with therapy, and I'm the first to admit it. One therapist pointed out that I couldn't one week be friendly and kind, the next be angry and hostile and the next sad, crying and stuck on the couch. She said I had to force myself to overcome this and be friendly and kind all the time. As much as this was true, the actions that come with those words were too hard to actually accomplish. I believe a lot of this had to do with me being wrongly medicated. How was one to put actions to the truthful words, how was I supposed to work through these difficulties if my brain was not stable enough to correct the problem? I am a firm believer that medication and stability must come before any type of therapy will be beneficial for us. That does not mean that going to a trained therapist, preferably one who specializes in bipolar patients, will not help you. Therapy can give you the tools you need to be using while you are waiting for the right medication combo. I believe this illness can be overcome. Finding a therapist, one you click with, one who can give you coping skills and teach them to you, one who can give you direction is the best kind. After you have reached stability it's time to find a therapist who can help you cope with the day-to-day stuff. Find a therapist who can help you to reality check and continue using the tools you have learned through directional therapy.

Routine and structure... consistency, are just a few things children thrive on. Throughout the years of me being a parent, my children have always done better and responded to me better when they knew exactly what to expect from me. Knowing what to expect also establishes a level of trust. They know your words mean something and are not going to be different tomorrow. It is always a good thing to stop and think before you snap. If you are snapping over something that wouldn't normally bother you, then it's something you need to let go. Do it even if that means taking that 10-minute-break to splash some cold water on your face, go outside for a breather, or lock yourself in the bathroom to take a few breaths for yourself. Protecting your children from your mental illness should be right at the top of your list.

As mentioned earlier, Joshy, or JP for short, has taken the brunt of my illness. There are many factors I believe have come into play here. I have ruminated over this fact for the better part of the time after being diagnosed and finally stable. JP was born just five weeks before my mom passed away. Although JP and I had an awesome connection, he loved me and I adored him with every part of my being, sometime after my mom's passing, I became distant. I can remember those first few days, just two weeks after his birth. I had two of my back teeth pulled. Between some PTSD, pregnancy and some really bad genes, my teeth have taken a really hard hit. Having those teeth pulled so early after he was born put a huge damper on JP's and my relationship. I was in excruciating pain for a very long time and found myself feeding him and then handing him off to Dan or my mom. I really didn't bond with him that well and we were drifting apart before he was even six-weeks-old. Then came the passing of my mom. This put a complete halt in my relationship with JP. As soon as the news spread that my mom had passed, my home was filled with grieving relatives and friends, all there to offer support and pick up the pieces that I was too broken to fix.

About a week after my mom's death, I gave up nursing JP entirely. This was probably my first mistake. I was dealing with postpartum depression, grieving my mother and the stress of getting my mom's house cleaned out before the holiday season. I cried every day, sometimes all day, especially once everyone was gone. This was the first time I ever went to see a psychiatrist for what I had been feeling. I was hoping that this time we would be able to get the depression under control with a different antidepressant. I was prescribed Prozac and Trazodone. Both of these meds together sent me straight into a manic episode. Soon my mom's house was completely cleaned out. I began baking cookies for the holidays and I would bake around the clock, thinking I had tons of people to give cookies to. I prepared for a huge Thanksgiving feast at our home. I cleaned around the clock while I waited for the cookies. And then... I impulsively decided to sign our home back to the bank and pack up the entire family and move to North Carolina. This put even more distance between JP and me as there was no time for me to give to him. I fed him, changed him and plopped him in his swing or bassinet. The move caused him disruption because of the home he was used to. Once I decided North Carolina wasn't going to work out, I again impulsively moved the family to Utah to be near my brother and when that didn't work out the way I had hoped, we moved back to Pennsylvania. All this moving happened in a matter of five months. Poor JP didn't know what stability was, and for that matter, neither did my other children. The first eight months of JP's life he spent either in a swing, a crib, a car seat driving all over the country, or in his bouncy seat. We stayed with friends for a while when we came back to Pennsylvania, but due to their home not being baby-proofed, I had JP in his playpen most of the time. Once we finally moved into our own home, the mania kicked in full force. I was non-stop for months and then took on the great idea of home schooling our older children. There was just no time for JP at all.

Then Macie made her appearance into this world. She was sick and a high-needs baby. I needed to put 90% of my time on her, 5% went to schooling the kids and the other 5%

was used to try to keep the house in some form of normality. A lot of fighting was going on with Dan and me. Money was tight, there were problems with another family member, and our lives were beginning to unravel. I spent virtually no time with JP or the other children. He fell through the cracks and I was too self-centered, too sick to even see it.

After Emmie was born and I was pregnant with Mollie, I hit one of the worst mixed states of my life. I was trying to potty train JP. He was four-years-old. He was way overdue, or so I thought. Thinking back, he really wasn't. It wasn't until he was 22-months-old when he walked, just about the same age before he really started talking. My patience were running thin, he was not progressing well and I did one of the worst things a parent could do. I yelled at him for having an accident. Duh! How counter-productive was that? I felt like such an asshole! I didn't deserve to be a mother. What kind of mother yells at her child for having a natural accident? It happens! This wasn't my first rodeo, what was wrong with me? Finally he got it. He picked up what he needed to do and we were all pleased, doing the happy dance. But I was still not under control, the medications had yet to start working and when he began regressing, I began getting verbally aggressive. I would yell at him and cut him down for having accidents. Afterwards I would feel so horrible. I would try to apologize for the way I acted, explaining I was wrong and cuddle him. Sometimes it worked, other times, he shied away from me. He had been through too much with me already, he was scared of me. One afternoon in late July 2011, JP had another accident. I grabbed his little hand, escorted him into the bathroom and yelled for I don't know how long about where he's supposed to go to the bathroom. As soon as I realized what I was doing, I stopped myself, took a step back, watched the look on his face change from confusion to fear and then I walked away, got him clean underwear and cleaned him up. After he was done in the bathroom, I locked myself in there and cried. It was the first time I had EVER been aggressive with my children and I hated myself for it. Sure, I apologized, but it wasn't enough. What was done was done. The damage had already been done and there was no going back. It wasn't long after that particular incident when I started thinking about killing myself again. I was toxic to my family, toxic to my kids and they didn't deserve for me to treat them that way. They deserved to have a mother who could love them in a way that I couldn't. They didn't deserve a mother with a mental illness. No, they deserved better. They never asked for a wacko mommy. No, they were innocent.

But this is where the sneaky devil of depression gets you. It lies to you and it makes you believe that you can't be a good parent, that you can't overcome the illness that has been dealt to you. It's a lie and it can be overcome. You can change. With medication, therapy and determination, things can be better for you and for your children. It's just a matter of having the resources, the tools to make it all happen, to make it all fit together. The afternoon after I snapped, I made an emergency call to my psychiatrist's office. I explained the situation and was given a med increase. I avoided JP all the more for fear that I'd do the same thing to him. I seriously considered inpatient, but thankfully the meds kicked in and suddenly the mixed episode was replaced with some semblance of normality. But that hasn't stopped JP's tentativeness around me. This was something none of the other children ever had with me and it does break my heart. It is something I am still working on and I work daily on giving him hugs and kisses, telling him how much I love him, walking away when things get to be too much for me. I can only hope that one day, he won't have to worry about me freaking out like that on him again.

In light of my last section of the book, I'd like to touch upon a very sensitive topic: *Should someone with a severe mental illness have children?* This is a question many of us have asked ourselves and one that has been raised in the media as well. Again, I think a lot of the questions being raised come from lack of information and people who are clueless as to how mental illness really works, and of how awesome an outcome one can have IF proper treatment is in place. Personally, I was not getting treated properly, but in a weird kind of way, I'm happy for that. Had I been getting treatment, my psychosis would have been under control and I probably wouldn't have had the seven wonderful kids I have today. I wouldn't have had seven reasons to keep on fighting. With treatment in place, moms and dads even with severe mental illnesses like bipolar and schizophrenia can be wonderful parents. Honestly, this is a very sensitive subject and a very personal decision. It's a decision that only you can make for yourself. A decision a couple should make together. It isn't something you can seek out an opinion on, because only you know what's best for you and what you think you can handle. I personally feel that anyone who wants to have children should have children. There's nothing that should stand in your way, even if it is a mental illness. All of those can be managed and overcome, allowing you to be the best parent possible. The question is always raised: *What if I pass the gene along?* My answer to this always is the same. Look back at your own family history. If there is anyone in your family with heart disease, diabetes or some other genetically inherited illness, you have the likelihood of passing that gene on to your children. If a medical condition such as those listed above is not enough to make you worry about passing on the gene, then why are you worrying about mental illness being passed along? Also, just because you have bipolar doesn't mean your child will have bipolar. The chances are only about 30%. That may sound like a lot, but you do have to consider the opposite side of this.

There's a 70% chance that the child will not inherit your illness. Those statistics sound pretty good to me. Ultimately the choice is yours. Do your research, talk with your psychiatrist and OB/GYN before-hand about your treatment and make sure you are stable before you get pregnant. Discuss treatment options and if your medications are safe. What meds could you potentially switch to so you can have a child? And remember to most definitely discuss this with your partner. His or her input matters just as much as how you feel about the situation. Have a plan in place before you have the baby just in case postpartum depression kicks in.

Chapter Nine

HAVING A CHILD of my own being diagnosed with a mental illness, I know how scary it is to think that something may be *wrong* with my child. The truth is, nothing is wrong with her, she is just different, just like you and I. Lizzie is a bubbly, smart and curious young lady. She will one day be a CEO of a company. She's very strong willed and has no problem stating her opinions and deciding that her way is the best way. It's her brain, like mine, that works in a much different way than other people. That may not be a terrible thing, especially if we get it under control now and help her learn how to cope and manager her symptoms. One in ten children are affected by mental illness, and most of those cases happen before the age of 14.

There are many different disorders that affect children. Some of them may be: attention deficit hyperactivity disorder, anxiety disorders, autism spectrum disorder, bipolar disorder, depression, eating disorders and schizophrenia. As you can see, these are the same disorders that affect adults as well. It is easier to diagnose an adult with any of these mental illnesses as an adult has the capability of expressing their feelings much better than a child. So how does a parent figure out if what is going on with their child is normal, everyday stuff or something a bit more?

- First and foremost, talk with your child's pediatrician. He or she will be able to evaluate your child for any possible medical explanation for your child's behavior. He will do a full physical workup and be able to order blood tests and other testing he may feel is necessary. This step is important and it will eliminate some of these tests being needed in the future. Provide your doctor with as much information as you possibly can. The more he knows, the better he can help your child. I wish we would have taken this step with Lizzie. It most likely would have avoided her traumatic hospitalization.

- Talk with your child's teacher. Your child's teacher spends a great deal of time with your child and may observe behaviors you are not seeing at home. Share your concerns with your child's teacher so they can be on the lookout for any potential issues they may have missed. Ask the teacher to report back to you and share these concerns with your child's doctor.

- If your child is cared for by anyone else while you or your spouse are working, speak with them as well. Report all information to your doctor.

Your pediatrician may refer your child to see a specialist. He or she may suggest therapy first. Sometimes the behavior your child is displaying is for a different reason than mental illness. It could be a behavioral issue that can be dealt with through therapy and teaching everyone in the family how to cope and manage those behavior issues. It could also be something as simple as adding a new sibling to the home. Maybe you have moved to a new house or area recently. Sometimes children begin to act out because they are unhappy about those things. They feel they are not getting enough attention or they don't handle change easily. You also may be referred to a child psychologist to have further psych evaluation done on your child. This does not necessarily mean anything is wonky in your child's brain; it is merely a tool to rule this possibility out. I remember when we first started therapy with Lizzie. I was a nervous wreck about the entire situation. I worried about what they may find, and I was right to worry. But in the end, I was happy she was getting the treatment she needed. Lizzie sees a therapist regularly now, and I think it has been beneficial for her. She is able to learn coping skills that are geared towards a child's way of thinking. There are a few types of other specialists you may be referred to. Some of them being: psychiatrists, social workers, psychiatric nurses or behavioral therapists, maybe even a neurologist. In some cases, you may be referred to all of these specialists. Again, there is no reason to jump to any conclusions. This is just a step that must be taken to rule out any possibilities or conditions that may be going on with your child. Another piece of advice, don't take your doctor's word for granted. Just because one doctor has ruled out or has ruled in favor of a particular condition, doesn't mean he is right. Investigate further, do your own research, and learn as much as you can. If you disagree, seek out a second opinion if you feel that's the right thing to do.

When having Joshy evaluated, the behavioral therapist automatically jumped to an ADHD diagnosis. Although I agreed with her, I did not agree with her approach. You just can't make that kind of diagnosis from a 30-minute observation. They put him in a room with toys he had never seen nor played with before. It was natural for him to jump from toy to toy and to investigate them all. That to me was not a fair assessment, so we put off working with her. We are now in the process of working with his regular pediatrician and a neurologist. Don't be afraid to interview potential specialists and make sure they have experience in handling children. If they don't, try to find one who does. We are currently faced with this problem ourselves. The neurologist that Josh will go see is not a pediatric neurologist. He specializes in adults. But because the waiting list is over a year long to see a pediatric specialist, we are willing to take the chance. As you can see, this can be especially difficult, but it is important in the care of your child. Find the specialist that is right for you AND your child. If your child isn't comfortable with his or her specialist, then you need to find out why this is and possibly find a new one.

Also, whatever specialist you do find, make sure he or she understands that you want to be involved in each and every aspect of your child's treatment. This does not mean that you want to sit in on every therapy session. Your child does deserve some privacy, and that privacy should be respected. What it does mean is the therapist is willing to answer your questions without breaking confidentiality of your child. It means the specialist is willing to help you learn how to cope and manage your child's symptoms. You want to know the results of EVERY test preformed on your child. Discuss treatment and medication options in-depth with the specialist before a final decision is made. Once your child has received a diagnosis, do like I have stressed a million times over about your own diagnosis. Educate yourself! If you know nothing about what is going on with your child, then you will not understand how best to help your child. Your child will run through the system, being bounced from specialist to specialist if you are unable to advocate for and stand by any decisions that have already been made concerning your child's treatment. You need to be able to understand exactly what is going on with your child and be able to accept that your child's diagnosis doesn't define him anymore than your diagnosis defines you.

So how do you know when it's time to seek help? Here are just a few tips:

- Problems in different areas of your child's life: home, school, friendships. From personal experience, there has to be a problem in two or more areas, one of them being outside the home environment.

- Changes in eating and sleeping habits: Either too much or too little. When Lizzie is not feeling well, it's hard to get her to eat. When she's manic, she craves sweets. It's a hard balance to keep up with, but we do try our very best.

- Social withdrawal. Sometimes this can be due to depression, or the child is isolated from his or her peers because their behavior becomes bothersome to other children. Lizzie is prone to outbursts and getting upset easily. This created some issues in making friends for quite a while.

- Fearful behavior towards things that your child isn't usually afraid of.

- Regression - Bed wetting, sucking thumb, sleeping with you at night. We've experienced all of this with both Lizzie and Joshy. Lizzie has stopped sucking her thumb and has moved back to her own bed. Joshy is still working on going all night without wetting the bed. We do have more good nights than bad, I will admit.

- Sadness, easily upset (especially over small things), tearfulness for no reason.

- Self-destructive behavior - head banging, a tendency to get hurt often, self-harm.

- Thoughts or remarks about death. All children have these kinds of questions. Death is something a child can't understand, so they may ask frequent questions. This is especially true after the death of a loved one. These questions can be normal, but when they are in combination with the list above, it's time to seek help.

Once a diagnosis is made, then you will be able to work towards treatment options for your child. I've already mentioned above some of the treatments that may be an option for your child. The main question is, what if your child needs medication? Ultimately, that decision is up to you. I can say from personal experience that a good psychiatrist is not going to put any child on medication right away. Good psychiatrists are not going to push pills at you, and they only use medications when they absolutely feel it is necessary. If medication is suggested, ask what kind and then ask for a follow-up appointment in a week before you decide if it's right for your child. This will give you enough time to do some research on the medication and find out for yourself if it's the right medication for your child. If you disagree with your doctor, discuss other medication options. Often medication is needed and absolutely necessary in helping to control and manage your child's symptoms. There's a lot of information out there promoting vitamins and healthy diet. Although those things are extremely important and can with your doctor's approval be used to help, they are not stand-alone treatment options of a mentally ill child and should not be used as such. I cannot urge you enough to go to a psychiatrist when you find that your child has a mental illness. As comfortable as you and your child may be with your pediatrician, they are not trained extensively in mental illnesses. They have a general overview of mental illness and will not be able to care for your child the way a psychiatrist can. Mental illness is a psychiatrist's specialty and they can help you the best. Too many times, I've made this mistake concerning myself. It only ended up in me being more frustrated and confused. It wasn't until I allowed a psychiatrist to do the job for me that I ended up getting the proper treatment.

One last thing, be patient. It can take a long time to get a proper diagnosis for your child, and even longer to find the right kind of combination of treatments. Things will not just happen overnight. Waiting for a diagnosis and how best to treat your child can be discouraging. Jumping too fast could be detrimental. Remember be patient and take your time, don't jump to conclusions and don't let the information you find scare you. We all know how difficult it is to be a bipolar parent. I hope some of the tips and suggestions I have offered to you will be of at least some help. Our job becomes much more difficult when we have a child who is also suffering with a mental illness, but that job is not impossible. I'd prefer to view it as I have the advantage here. I already understand my daughter's thoughts, actions, behaviors and feelings. I can identify with her and she's able to come to me and talk about how she feels because she knows I already understand. You, too, have that advantage if you are raising a bipolar child. Getting your child the proper treatment that he or she needs should be your first line of duty. This includes working closely with a psychiatrist who is skilled in pediatrics. The next step is making sure your child is working with a therapist. Again, the therapist should be specially trained to handle bipolar children. Once your child is diagnosed there will be a lot of questions both you and your child may have. Make a list of those questions and take them with you to your child's next psychiatry appointment.

You may be wondering how best to help your child, and that's where the therapy comes in. It can help you to identify what is your child's normal behavior versus times of depression or mania. Children are more prone to rapid cycling, meaning they are fine in the morning, depressed by the afternoon and manic by the time they are ready to go to bed. Sometimes these moods can cycle within hours of each other. Raging outbursts are not uncommon and can last anywhere from 30 minutes to hours depending upon the child.

When Lizzie is feeling extra aggressive she will lash out just once at the closest person standing next to her. She will take her punishment, storm off to her room, slamming chairs, tipping chairs, slamming doors and throwing whatever is in her way as she makes her way to her bedroom. As the door closes behind her you can hear her letting all her frustrations out in the privacy of her own room. She's there, in her own quiet space and it is there that she can vent out how she's feeling in pretty much any way she chooses, minus holes in walls or furniture. She typically cleans her closet out and hides in the back of it with her journal and her blanket. After a meltdown she likes to be left alone for a while. Part of this is due to embarrassment and the other part is due to her needing to cool off. Teaching her the cutoff point between a little bit mad and too much angry has been challenging, but we are making progress. She has fewer outbursts now that I've been teaching her some coping skills.

When diagnosed with bipolar disorder, medication is the first priority in treating the illness. This applies to children as well, but if the child does not learn how to cope and manage his or her illness, the problem will only get bigger. I believe all the parenting skills that are used to parent a child without a mental illness should be applied to parenting a child with a mental illness. In our home we still issue time outs, loss of privileges and groundings. No child is disciplined any differently. In my opinion, if Lizzie doesn't get in trouble for flipping the garbage can when she's mad and Andrew does get into trouble, what lesson have I just taught both of them? Besides, when our bipolar children have grown into bipolar adults, the consequences will remain the same for them as any other citizen in the community. Our goal is to teach our children how to cope with their symptoms during, after and before an episode rears its ugly head. If your child is armed with the proper treatment, medication, therapist AND coping skills, then the outcome for your child is not going to be as poor as the child who has learned no coping skills.

Once your child learns of his or her diagnosis, they may have many questions they want to ask you. Some of them may be easy for you to answer as you are already living the life they are just starting. Being a bipolar parent gives you the advantage in being able to understand your child and help them to understand their illness for themselves. First and foremost, before you answer any of your child's questions, make sure they understand that their illness is NOT their fault and they did nothing to cause this to happen to them. Here are a few questions you may be faced with:

- *"Will it ever go away?"* You really have no definite answer here. Right now, that answer is no. But advances in medicine, science and technology may one day turn this answer into a yes. Explain here to your children how medication and therapy can help them to control their symptoms, but there is no cure for their illness. This is a good time to start talking about coping skills with your child.

- *"Is it contagious? How did I get this?"* No, we all know it is not contagious; no one can catch bipolar disorder because someone sneezed on them. How to answer the second part of this question is easier than you think. A simple response; *"Just as you got your blue eyes from Daddy, your nose from Nanny and your toes from Pappy, you got bipolar disorder from Mommy or Daddy."* (Whichever applies to the situation) Bipolar Disorder is just one of the many different types of illnesses that can and do run in families.

- *"How will medication help me?"* This sounds simple to answer, but it's not. After explaining how the medication will help them with their moods, will help them sleep and in some cases help them to not hear or see those scary things anymore, you may end up with more questions.

Questions about ....How? Just let them know that the medication will help their brain work a little better so that it can help the rest of their bodies work better, too. This seemed to pacify Lizzie.

There are also many books about childhood bipolar disorder you can get from your library, online bookstores, and there's a free PDF download on DBSA's website geared towards children. I actually printed this one out recently and shared it with Lizzie. It helped her understand her illness a lot better than I could have even explained it to her. Let's go over a few ways you can help your child learn how to cope with their illness.

Ways to Help Your Child Cope:

- Make sure they understand that they are not alone, that there are other children suffering from the same disorder they have. Share your own story with them if you feel comfortable. Lizzie knowing I have days like she has made it a bit easier for her to come and talk to me. She knows I understand. At the same time, I've become the person she takes her anger out on, probably because she knows I don't take it personally. It's not her, it's her illness.

- Help your child find the line between being a little angry and aggressive angry. This may mean you have to catch your child a few times, giving them gentle reminders when you see they are beginning to get too angry. Don't be discouraged if your child doesn't respond well to your encouragement. They will probably be angry with you for calling them out on it. But if you want your child to grow up to be responsible for their mental health, this is an important step and coping skill they need to learn. I promise, one day they will thank you.

- Help your child find non-violent ways to express their feelings. Lizzie loves to draw pictures and write in her journal. This is an outlet for her to get all her negative feelings out on paper. I have also encouraged Lizzie that if she feels like hitting someone or something to go beat up her pillows instead. Releasing some of that aggression built up in her can be quite freeing and soon she's laughing because she sees how ridiculous the entire process is. Sometimes when Lizzie is having a terrible day, she and I go for a short walk. Just removing her from the situation is enough for her to get her head on straight and come back with apologies for whoever she was angry with.

- Encourage your child to talk to you and your spouse about how they are feeling. If you know what kind of feelings your child is having, the better you can help them cope with those feelings.

- Give your child a journal and tell him or her it is their own private space to write down how they feel or draw pictures in. This can be wonderful therapy for anyone. Sometimes just writing about their day can make them feel better.

- Make sure your child understands the importance of being honest with their doctors. Their doctors cannot help them if they don't know how your child is feeling.

- Most importantly, make sure your child knows that if they feel like hurting themselves, they must tell you or another trusted adult right away - that you won't be angry with them and that this is a symptom of their illness and it needs medical attention. Stress this as much as possible without downplaying the importance of it.

Ways to Help Your Child Manage Their Illness:

- Teach your child to chart her moods and symptoms. If she or he is old enough, after learning, she can do this on her own. I would encourage you to also keep track of your child's symptoms for your own records. When symptomatic, it's hard to have insight into ourselves. This will fill in any blanks when it's time to visit your child's psychiatrist or therapist.

- Be in control of your child's medications. I wouldn't suggest allowing a bipolar child to control their own medication at all. It's just too much of a risk to take in doing this.

- Teach your child coping mechanisms: walking away when they feel angry, writing in their journal, humming to themselves, going to a quiet space when she or he feels agitated or angry, punching pillows instead of walls or other people.

Bipolar children are and can be very successful. Help them understand this by pointing out famous people who have overcome their bipolar disorder and redirected their energies into something they love. Help your children find their inner talents, their skills, the things that they are passionate about. Then....provide them with the resources necessary so they may continue being passionate about whatever they choose. This may be a place of safety for them, a place for them to unwind, something to do to take their mind off of the illness they have to contend with every day of their lives. Encourage them, tell them how awesome of a job they are doing and last, but absolutely not least, **SHOW THEM YOU LOVE THEM ALL THE TIME!** I also suggest keeping a journal of your child's behavior for yourself. This is not a place where you write about how you feel about your child, but a place to track his or her moods, behaviors you are observing, medications your child is taken, medications your child cannot take or medications that have not worked for your child. You can keep this in a folder with all your child's information in it: medical, psychiatric, insurance, notes you've taken, records from the doctor, appointments, even a weekly journal of how you observed your child's week and what stressors may have contributed to a bad or good week. You can bring this information with you to all of your child's doctor appointments and have it handy in the event a hospitalization is necessary.*

As mentioned earlier, psychosis can and does happen with a bipolar diagnosis. When a child experiences psychosis, it is often as scary to them if not more so than it is to us. Psychosis is a mental disorder characterized by symptoms, such as delusions or hallucinations that indicate impaired contact with reality. Now try explaining that to a child! Here I hope I can help you come up with some ways of doing just that! Explaining to your child the different elements of psychosis can prove to be quite difficult. For example, hallucinations can be particularly difficult, because the child most likely firmly believes that what they are seeing and hearing is real. They may not realize that the hallucinations they are experiencing are not really there. If your child knows they aren't real, explaining the disorder will be easier. But first you must tackle the "*they are real*" part. In order to do that, you must be working with a psychiatrist to get those symptoms under control. After symptom control is in place it would be good for both you and your psychiatrist to sit down with your child and come up with a plan on how they could tell you what they are seeing and hearing. Explaining to your child that these are just hallucinations, they are not real and they cannot hurt you is better saved for when your child is well and can understand you better. Do not argue with your child about these hallucinations, simply pick up the phone and call their psychiatrist and get them in for a medication adjustment. Sometimes medication is not enough to make all hallucinations go away and you'll need to work with your child, the psychiatrist and the child's therapist on coming up with ways to cope with these hallucinations. One thing that has always helped me is to ask if anyone else just saw what I saw. If collectively that answer is no, then I know what's going on with me, especially if this has happened more than once. The same advice could be given to your own child, but be careful. You don't want her asking friends, and then having the situation get out of control. Ask her to only ask people who know and understand her situation.

Next you will need to tackle the *"Why am I seeing and hearing things that aren't there?"* question. I suggest comparing it to sicknesses like the flu or a cold. Help them to understand that they have an illness in their brain, just like we get illnesses in our tummies or our chests. Explain that this illness affects the part of the brain that controls our emotions and the way we think and behave sometimes. Make sure they understand that it's not their fault and it's nothing they should feel guilty about. Also, letting them know the name of their illness is important when explaining the disorder to them. If they are just told they are sick in the brain, that isn't going to answer much for them. Teaching your child what symptoms to watch out for will be extremely helpful to both you and your child. If both of you can track her symptoms together, then you are teaching a life skill. Your child is also learning how to manage their own illness. You will also be able to gauge how well your child is doing and if a call to the psychiatrist is in order. Lizzie and I both use a website called patientslikeme.com. It's pretty involved, but it works for us. There are many other trackers out there or you can make one of your own. Be sure to let your child know that if the voices ever tell him or her to hurt themselves or to harm others, they need to tell you or another trusted adult immediately. This is a symptom of their illness and it needs immediate attention. Just like a fever needs to be taken care of so it doesn't get too high, so does this symptom. I would suggest having a plan in place with your child's psychiatrist in the event that this happens. Different doctors approach this differently. Answer all and every question your child has. Be as open and honest with your child as you can be. If you don't know the answer, tell them you will find out that answer for them. Then call the psychiatrist or therapist and find the answer to their questions. Some children who fall on the bipolar spectrum are able to lead independent lives. They may be able to go through school okay, go to college and be successful. However, there is another side to this, where that thought is impossible. Planning for the future is important.

Planning For the Future:

- Have custody arrangements set into place and legalized. In the event that you or your spouse is unable to care for your child, for whatever reason, this step is important. You don't want your child to be institutionalized if it can be avoided.

- Take out a life insurance policy - One on yourself and one on your child.

- Have a bank account set up that can be turned over to your child when they are older. This account could also be transferred to your child's appointed guardian if need be.

- Some children who have been diagnosed with a severe mental illness qualify for Social Security Income, or SSI. These benefits can help curb the cost of raising your child or it can be tucked away into that savings account for when your child is older.

Whatever you do, don't forget your child is still your child. Hug them, kiss them and tell them often how much you love them. Let them know you are there for them and that they can talk to you about anything and everything.

If you have other children, you have the added responsibility of explaining to them what is happening with their sibling. I would suggest talking with them in private. Use the same words and terms as you used to explain it to the child who is sick. This disorder is not just yours and your spouse's issue, it affects the entire family. Help them to know that they do not need to be afraid of their sibling nor are they to be embarrassed of them. They should also not feel guilty for the way they may have treated them in the past. Just as you were open and honest in answering their sibling's questions, be the same way with your other children. They may be curious and concerned and want to know more about what's going on or how they can help. Involve your older children in treatments, the disorder's progression, and long-term care options. They may one day be their sibling's caregiver and they will need to know their sibling's history. I would also explain to your older children that this illness is genetic.

Chapter Ten

TO THINK recovery is impossible is to have no hope, and hope is something I hold onto even when I'm at the bottom of despair. Recovery is absolutely possible, but it's different for everyone. Not everyone will recover at the same pace as someone else. While it may take one person only a few months to bounce back from an episode, it can take another person a year or more. I believe recovery is the hardest part of the pole we swing. Each time you reach the recovery process, remember, it gets easier. When you find yourself right smack in the middle of an episode, remind yourself that IT WILL GET BETTER! It did before and it will again, even if it doesn't feel like it right now. My definition of recovery may be much different than yours. For me, recovery means I can go back to being a mom. I can play with my kids, read them bedtime stories, give them baths, run around outside with them, go for walks with them, hum and sing to my babies. It means I am interested and invested in their lives. I invest all I have into them. It means that they don't have to see me sulking in bed or on the couch or hear me snipping and snapping at them for making messes that all children do. It means that I ENJOY my children and view them as the blessings they are to my life. They are the precious little gifts the stork dropped off on our stoop and into my heart. It also means that I can be a wife again. I can enjoy date nights with Dan, even if it is just a movie here at home after the kids go to bed, or a late night meal - just the two of us. It means Dan can make me laugh again and smile and giggle like he could when I was 15-years-old. It means that I would throw myself in front of a train for him, not because I want to die, but because I want him to LIVE.

It means I can enjoy just being me. I can go back to writing, something I love to do. I can reach out to others and help them through a difficult time. I can enjoy my hobbies like cross-stitching, journaling, blogging or some other crafty project. It also means I can enjoy music again, a true passion of mine. I can feel the music without all the wonky gunk of my brain getting in the way. I am LIVING! And that's what it should mean for all of us. Living, not just merely surviving or just waiting in doom for the next episode to take us over. It means living in the moment and enjoying every precious part of the good times you are having. There is no right or wrong way to recover. How it happens is up to you.

Chapter Eleven

JUST BECAUSE we have been labeled, and that label says "bipolar" does not mean we cannot be good parents. We must overcome life's hurdles, the episodes, the depression, the mania and be the best parents we can be. I believe that recovery is possible for all of us. It's up to us, individually, to figure out how we are going to combat the demon that stands lurking in the shadows. We do not have to let this illness control our lives. It is within us and of our power to take control of it. If we put forth the energy and take the steps to ensure our episodes are short and infrequent we can go on to be as good as any other parent out there.

I have always showed signs of bipolar disorder, even from my early teens. I can still remember my first full-blown manic episode at the age of 13, but no one really knew what was going on with me or how to deal with it. So like most things that my family found complicated and ashamed of, it was pushed under the carpet. For years I lived a semi "normal" life. Most of my issues were chalked up to me being a typical teenager, or a rebellious teen because my parents had just separated and were heading toward divorce. Everyone thought my behavior was a reflection of my home life. The truth was, a mental illness was brewing inside of me and eating me alive. It wasn't until I was pregnant with our seventh child before I finally broke into one of the worst depressions of my life. I had just given birth to our sixth baby, not four months prior, and was feeling the effects of pregnancy hormones, postpartum depression and full-blown psychosis. I became increasingly paranoid about everyone and everything around me. So paranoid, I wouldn't even let my children play outside and enjoy their summer vacation. I kept everything locked up tight and all the curtains and windows drawn for fear "somebody" might see or hear us inside. I was certain I was being monitored, by who? I didn't know.

I was just about four months pregnant when I began to contemplate suicide and my Hubs had to rush me to the ER. I begged them to allow me to come home to my six babies waiting for me and reluctantly they agreed. I was set up with psychiatric care and a good therapist. In less than a month I went from being a ball of hormones to receiving an official diagnosis of bipolar 1 disorder. I was shocked and I argued with the doctor. I didn't believe it was possible. I thought for sure it was just hormones. But he made me promise to go home and do my own research and if I found any evidence to prove him wrong, we'd discuss a different diagnosis. The truth was, I couldn't find any holes in his story once I started educating myself.

I walked in the following week with an entirely different attitude and I was ready to start whatever treatments he had in mind. He consulted with my OB first and we went from there, starting on a low dose of Seroquel and working my way up to a therapeutic level. It wasn't until I hit around 400mg before I started feel a sense of normalcy come back into my life. I wasn't miraculously cured, but my perspective on things brightened just a little bit. I firmly believe I fall somewhere in the middle of postpartum depression and postpartum bipolar disorder. Although I showed signs much sooner in my teens, it took having two pregnancies so close together to bridge the gap and have the disorder close in on me. This is a topic I know quite well, mainly because I was diagnosed with bipolar disorder just four short months after the birth of our sixth child. They could have diagnosed me as having postpartum depression, but I was already pregnant with our seventh child at the time, so I was given a diagnosis of bipolar 1 disorder.

I still remember those early days, before I was diagnosed. I often cried for no apparent reason and I only held Emmie long enough to feed her and then passed her off to whoever was willing to tend to her emotional needs. I felt overwhelmed by the tasks that laid in front of me and I felt inadequate as a mother. I didn't realize that I was experiencing psychosis and that the voices that were talking down to me were not really there. I still to this day can remember all the negative things they said to me and what they almost drove me to do. If it had not been for a wonderful psychiatric team and my husband, I have no doubt that neither Mollie nor myself would be here today. I believe that I had what is now known as postpartum bipolar disorder. The birth of my sixth child triggered postpartum depression and when I ended up pregnant just ten weeks after Emmie's birth the bipolar was thrown into full swing.

I recently read an article on PsychCentral.com and learned that women treated for postpartum depression should be screened for bipolar disorder as well. I couldn't agree with this statement more. Had someone screened me back in 2001 I would have been given the proper diagnosis many years before I was actually diagnosed with bipolar, and treatment could have been underway. Considering that bipolar is more likely to end in suicide, I would think that this would be on the top priority list of symptoms doctors should be screening for. It is very likely that a woman who has suffered from postpartum depression could develop bipolar disorder after she has had her baby. I was depressed through much of my pregnancy with Emmie and therefore I was at a higher risk for postpartum depression. The two pregnancies being so close together was an explosion of hormones just waiting to happen.

Once I was in touch with a good treatment team, I was able to start my journey to the road of stability. It would be three years before I would find some common ground that I could call balanced enough to be stability. It took many medication trials and errors and many different hospital stays before I could get to the point where I am at today. The sad part is, if doctors would just screen for more than postpartum depression more mothers would be getting the help they need and there would be less tragic loss in the end. I myself have experienced both postpartum depression and postpartum bipolar disorder and had I not been keen to my own senses, I wouldn't have realized I needed to reach out for help. Unfortunately, we live in a society where reaching out for mental help is considered a weakness. Women and men alike should be encouraged to take care of their mental health just like they take care of their physical health. We must band together and start raising awareness so we can give all parents a fighting chance at survival.

MORE GREAT READS
FROM BOOKTROPE

Broken Pieces **by Rachel Thompson** (Memoir / Essay) Vastly different in tone from her previous essay collections A Walk In The Snark and The Mancode: Exposed, BROKEN PIECES is an award-winning collection of pieces inspired by one woman's life: love, loss, abuse, trust, grief, and ultimately, love again.

My Fluorescent God **by Joe Guppy** (Memoir) In 1979, 23-year-old Joe Guppy was struggling with a bad breakup, but a few stomach pills drove him into paranoid psychosis… and straight into a mental ward. This raw, often comic memoir is a powerful spiritual and psychological adventure.

Memoirs Aren't Fairytales **by Marni Mann** (Contemporary Fiction) Leaving her old life behind, Nicole finds herself falling deeper and deeper into heroin addiction. Can she ever find her way back to a life free of track marks? Does she even want to?

American Goulash **by Stephanie Yuhas** (Memoir / Humor) A story about a nerd girl jousting with her Transylvanian family on the battlefields of suburban New Jersey for a chance to grow up authentically awkward and live a so-called normal American life.

Discover more books and learn about our
new approach to publishing at **booktrope.com**.

21440918R00067

Made in the USA
San Bernardino, CA
20 May 2015